Woodpecker Wars

Celebrating the Spirituality of Everyday Life

Peter DeHaan, PhD

Woodpecker Wars: Celebrating the Spirituality of Everyday Life
© 2019 by Peter DeHaan.

All rights reserved: No part of this book may be reproduced, disseminated, or transmitted in any form, by any means, or for any purpose without the express written consent of the author or his legal representatives. The only exception is the cover image and short excerpts for reviews or academic research.

Scriptures taken from the Holy Bible, New International Version®, NIV®. Copyright © 1973, 1978, 1984, 2011 by Biblica, Inc.™ Used by permission of Zondervan. All rights reserved worldwide. www.zondervan.com The "NIV" and "New International Version" are trademarks registered in the United States Patent and Trademark Office by Biblica, Inc.™

ISBNs:

    978-1-948082-23-5 (e-book)

    978-1-948082-24-2 (paperback)

    978-1-948082-25-9 (hardcover)

Published by Spiritually Speaking Publishing

Credits:

    Developmental editor: Erin K. Brown

    Copy editor/proofreader: Robyn Mulder

    Cover design: Cassia Friello

    Author photo: Chele Reagh/PippinReaghDesign

*To our children, Laura and Chris,
Dan and Kelli.*

No woodpeckers were harmed in the writing of this book.

Contents

Let's Get Started 1
1. Family 3
    I Never Did Propose 4
    The Queen of Desserts 6
    The Long and Short of It 7
    Just Say Yes 9
    Praying for My Children 11
    A Presumptive Question 15
    How Many Kids Do You Have? 17
    Friday Night Pizza 18
    Easter Communion 20
    Every Family Is Special 22
    One Kid or Two? 24
2. Holidays 27
    I Heart You Day 28
    Celebrating St Patrick's Day 30
    What's Good about Good Friday? 32
    Resurrection Sunday (aka Easter) 34
    Happy Thanksgiving! 36
    Our Christmas 37

Your Christmas	39
Their Christmas	40
Happy New Year!	41
Have a Happy Normal Day	43

3. Seasons Change 45
Four Seasons	46
Summertime	48
So Long, Summer	50
Fall Has Fallen	51
Winter Is Here	53
Spring Has Sprung	54
Celebrate the Seasons	56

4. God's Creation 57
Let's Take a Walk	58
An Unexpected Encounter	60
Why Recycle When You Can Refuse?	62
Save a Tree	64
Going Paperless	65
More Than Walking	67

5. Gardening 69
Pursuing Green	70
April Showers Bring May Flowers	72
Time to Move the Sprinklers	74
A Micro Garden	76
The Last Yard Work for the Season	78
Then We Moved	79

6. Weather 81
It's That Time of Year	82
Lake-Effect Snow	83

Let It Snow! 84
Unseasonably Warm 85
Weathering the Storm 86
The Comings and Goings of Toads 87
This Is for the Birds 89

7. Wildlife 91
Woodpecker Wars 92
Oh, Deer! 94
The Birds 96
The Power of Panic 98
Birdbrain Behavior 99
Feeding Rabbits 101
Raccoons in the Neighborhood 102
The Return of the Woodpeckers 104
Animal Rescue 106
Squirrelly Behavior 108
Crazy Rabbits 110
The Woodpeckers Strike Back 111
Where Do Frogs Come From? 112
A Lesson on Compassion 113
Then We Moved 115

8. Health 117
The Effects of the Flu 118
Do You Lie to Your Doctor? 119
The Christmas Five 121
Time Lag 123
Find Time to Slow Down? 126
The Stress of Time 128
My Routine 130

9. Work 135
- I Love My Job 136
- Pursuing a Forty-Hour Workweek 139
- The Birds Are Singing 141
- There Has to Be a Better Way 142
- Partner or Employee? 144
- Six Years Too Late 146
- Checkmate 148
- Can You Disconnect? 150
- I Can't Wait to Go to Work 152
- I Am a Writer 154
- Why I Write 156

10. Money 157
- How Much Is Enough? 158
- Living Beneath Your Means 159
- Are You Wealthy? 161
- We Must Change Our Attitude toward Money 163
- Needs Versus Wants 165
- End Poverty 167
- Trust God 169
- Blessed to Be a Blessing 170

11. Travel 171
- Three Stories about Flying 172
- Travel Mode 176
- Breakfast in Seattle 178
- Save Water 180
- Waiting for Sand 182

    Making Travel Connections......................... 183
    Who's in Control?.. 185
12. Personal... **187**
    Age Is Not a Number but an Attitude 188
    Cross Words... 190
    Flipping Houses 192
    Break Needless Habits 194
    The Third Time's the Charm....................... 196
    How Much Does It Cost?............................. 198
    Black and White in a Technicolor World ... 199
    How Many Friends Do You Have? 201
    A Picture Is Worth a Thousand Words 202
    How Secure Are Those Security
    Questions? 203
13. Pursuing Competence.. **205**
    Words Can Tear Down or Build Up 206
    A College Education for Everyone 208
    Road Rage.. 210
    A Reliable Witness 212
    My Mailbox Dilemma 213
    Haste Makes Waste 215
    Fire 216
    The Mathematics of Influence 218
14. Serious Stuff **219**
    Absolutes or Absolution? 220
    A Sad Situation 222
    With Freedom of Speech Comes

    Responsibility 223
    Homeless Statistics 224
    Avoid Poverty 226
    An Epic Fail 228
    What Does Pro-Life Mean? 229
    Set the Prisoners Free................................. 231
    Facts for the Fatherless 233
    Clean Water... 234
    Feed the Hungry.. 235
    Do Something 236

Final Thoughts 237
    The Bible.. 238
    What about Church? 241
    The Last Word... 243

Discussion Questions.. 244

Bonus Content: What Does Postmodern Mean? 246

Acknowledgments 249

About Peter DeHaan... 250

Other Books by Peter DeHaan

Check out Peter's other books:
The Dear Theophilus series:
- *Dear Theophilus: A 40-Day Devotional Exploring the Life of Jesus through the Gospel of Luke*
- *Dear Theophilus, Acts: 40 Devotional Insights for Today's Church*
- *Dear Theophilus, Isaiah: 40 Prophetic Insights about Jesus, Justice, and Gentiles*
- *Dear Theophilus, Minor Prophets: 40 Prophetic Teachings about Unfaithfulness, Punishment, and Hope*
- *Dear Theophilus, Job*

The 52 Churches series:
- *52 Churches: A Yearlong Journey Encountering God, His Church, and Our Common Faith*
- *The 52 Churches Workbook: Becoming a Spiritual Community that Matters*

- *More Than 52 Churches: The Journey Continues* (a sequel to *52 Churches*)
- *The More Than 52 Churches Workbook*

The Bible Bios series:
- *Women of the Bible: The Victorious, the Victims, the Virtuous, and the Vicious*
- *Friends and Foes of Jesus: Explore How People in the New Testament React to God's Good News*

Other books:
- *95 Tweets: Celebrating Martin Luther in the 21st Century*
- *How Big is Your Tent? A Call for Christian Unity, Tolerance, and Love*

Be the first to hear about Peter's new books and receive updates when you sign up at PeterDeHaan.com/updates

Let's Get Started

Once upon a time, people embraced the supernatural. They didn't split their reality into the physical and spiritual. This went beyond interconnecting these two perspectives. It wasn't even two sides of the same coin. It was one holistic reality. To them every aspect of life was divine.

Then humans got smart—or so they thought. They applied reason to their reality. They separated what they could observe, explain, and quantify from the abstract and mysteriousness of the sacred. They divided their existence into perceptible and ethereal. They separated secular from spiritual and ordered their lives accordingly.

The physical realm—the secular—celebrated the tangible. It occupied most of their conscious reality. People relegated the heavenly-focused aspect of life to Sunday mornings and a few other select times, if at all. They became enlightened—or not so much.

Yet today we witness a renewed interest in the otherworldly. People are increasingly open to the supernatural, the intangible reality that transcends our material world. For many, the divide between secular and sublime is vanishing. They, like me, see a hallowed element in every aspect of their lives. They're reclaiming the notion that every part of life has a revered component. It's a renaissance of reality, commingling the physical realm with the ethereal.

This book celebrates that renaissance.

Join me in celebrating the everyday spiritual aspects that make up my life. Then you can embark on a journey of rediscovering the everyday spirituality of yours.

1.

Family

He and all his family were devout and God-fearing; he gave generously to those in need and prayed to God regularly (Acts 10:2).

May Luke's description of the God-fearing centurion motivate us to lead our families well and cherish them as God's gift to us. Here's some of my story.

I Never Did Propose

Grandpa was an endearing nickname the church had given to one of our elder members. He looked like a grandpa and acted like a grandpa, albeit in a quirky yet winsome way. He often spoke before he thought, and he spoke a lot. Sometimes socially inappropriate, his words often embarrassed others. But the church loved him anyway because we had no doubt that he loved us.

One Sunday he marched up to me and my new girlfriend. He got right to the point. With a sly smile, he opened his mouth. "So, when you two getting married?"

I don't remember if I blushed, but this was certainly a blush-worthy moment. I took the initiative to deflect his impertinent question.

I gave a half-hearted smile. "We've only been dating a few months."

Our interaction continued, but I don't recall a single word he said after that. I just wanted to get out of there—fast. Eventually, we did. I tried to forget the whole conversation, but I was alone in that effort.

Though my girlfriend didn't mention it for a couple of weeks, she blurted her thoughts during a lull in conversation as we drove down the road. "So, you think Grandpa's going to get us married?"

I should've known this awkward question would come up again. I should've prepared a response. I hadn't.

I gulped in a lungful of courage. "Yeah, I suppose so."

Sheesh. How romantic.

We went shopping for rings a couple of weeks later.

I never did propose, and I never asked her parents for permission. I'm not sure if parents expected it back then, or if I didn't have enough common sense to do it. Not that it mattered much. We would have gotten married anyway.

At the time, we felt so mature, so ready. Looking back, we were so young, so unprepared.

Yet through the highs and lows that every marriage faces, God was with us. He blessed us with a marriage that lasts.

The Queen of Desserts

Each Christmas, my bride—whom early in our marriage I nicknamed the Queen of Desserts—goes on a Christmas baking frenzy. It's one of the ways she, and we along with her, celebrate Jesus. The preliminary round usually starts on a Saturday or her day off, but it continues for several days after.

She feigns irritation, but secretly enjoys my hovering, waiting to snatch the first piece of each batch as it's finished. Sometimes one sample isn't enough to judge the overall quality. In these instances, I need to try a second piece . . . and a third if I can get away with it. If she looks away, a fourth sample may disappear as well, but let's keep that as our secret.

Since I'm a morning person and she's a night owl, I often go to bed while she's still baking. This means that late at night I'm not available to let her know just how good each item is. Without my acute taste buds to assist, how will she know that the results meet her exacting standards? I'm not sure how she manages without my much-needed assistance, but I do know that the next day I'll resume my role as taste tester. It makes me hungry just thinking about it.

The Long and Short of It

Sometimes after a day at work, my bride comes home and says, "It's been a long day!"

Being the supportive spouse that I am, I respond with appropriate empathy. Unfortunately, I'm seldom content to merely agree, so I add, "Yes, I heard on the news that today was thirty-five minutes longer than yesterday. Today was truly a long day."

That rarely wins me any points, but does garner an irritated glare.

What she means is that work lasted—or seemed to last—a long time. Or it could convey that work was frustrating. I know what she means, but she doesn't say what she means. Instead, she insists that the day was longer than normal.

Likewise, some people quip that the summer solstice is the longest day of the year. That isn't correct either. It's the same length as all the others. It merely contains more daylight minutes—and correspondingly fewer nighttime minutes—than any other day of the year. That is, for those of us north of the equator.

For those in the Southern Hemisphere, our summer solstice—their winter solstice—is their shortest day of the year. Not really. It just has the least amount of daylight and the maximum amount of darkness.

What about those on the equator? They enjoy an even twelve-twelve split of light and dark, just like every other day.

Whether your day was long—or short—or the same length as all others, I hope it was a good one. Mine was.

Thank you, Jesus!

Just Say Yes

When our kids were in elementary school, I noticed that whenever they asked permission to do something, the default answer my wife and I gave was invariably, "No." Although we might eventually turn a few of those into yeses, most of the time we said no for no good reason. This realization convicted me of a need to change.

I apologized to our kids for saying no to them too often. I explained that going forward, I would use new guidelines to make a decision. In only three situations would I tell them no. The first was to keep them safe, the second was to keep them healthy, and the third was to help them learn what was right. For everything else I pledged to say yes.

They were incredulous. But the gleam in their eyes as they exchanged looks told me they would soon test my promise. A few days later they did just that.

They bounded up to me, brimming with mirth and bouncing with excitement. "Dad, can we go outside and run around barefoot in the snow?"

I smiled. "Sure! Have fun."

This shocked them. But they wasted no time throwing off their shoes and socks, pulling on winter coats, hats, and gloves, and running outside.

My bride was aghast, but they were gone before she could swoop in and intervene.

We were still engaged in an animated discussion about the wisdom of my decision when they came back inside forty-five seconds later with broad smiles and cold feet. They never asked to run barefoot in the snow again.

Going forward, I said yes every chance I got. I determined to be a parent who would say yes and let them encounter a wide swath of life and not be a parent who said no too often and stifle their opportunities to live large.

May we strive to say yes every chance we get.

Many people see God as poised to tell them no on everything, stifling their fun. But I suspect God wants to tell us yes as often as possible. And when he says no, it's to keep us safe, keep us healthy, and help us learn what is right.

Praying for My Children

Ever since our daughter was born, I knew I should pray for her, as well as for her brother, when he came along. I did pray for them—when I thought of it—which wasn't very often. I felt guilty for not doing what I knew I should do. And when I did pray, my prayers were always the same. My words repeated. They felt stale. When it came to praying for our kids, I was stuck in a rut.

When the oldest was in middle school, her youth group leader gave us a handout. Titled "Things I Pray for My Children," it listed twenty-three items to guide our prayers. I began praying one item each day. At the end of twenty-three days (or a little bit longer if I missed a day) I started the list over and prayed through it again, making one request each day.

The prayer list empowered me to pray for our children. I no longer felt guilty about neglecting this aspect of their spiritual development.

After a few years, however, the list had grown stale. Though I continued to pray, I began to struggle. About that time, I came across another list, a prayer card: "31 Biblical Virtues to Pray for Your Kids." This one had thirty-one suggestions, one for each day of a thirty-one-day month. Though both lists had similarities, no items were an exact duplicate. I now had thirty-one new ideas to guide my prayers.

On the months with thirty-one days, I used the thirty-one-day list. On the other months, I used the twenty-three-item list. And when I had run out of items for those months, I went off the list and came up with my own things to pray for our kids.

As they got older, I added their best friends to the list too. I did this because their friends were emerging as a bigger influence in their lives than their mom and me. I wanted their friends to be godly influences, so I prayed for them.

When they started dating, I prayed for those they were dating. One dated a lot and the other not so much. In college, I added their roommates.

Though the makeup of the list changed over time, the two people I consistently prayed for were our kids. Because I prayed for the people they were dating, their future spouses received years of prayer before they were engaged, even before they met.

These simple prayers, offered daily, one prayer at a time, were huge.

After they were married and the prospect of grandchildren became more realistic, I took a step of faith and began praying for their future children, my future grandchildren. Using the same two prayer lists to guide me, I prayed for God's blessing on what would be.

As each grandchild was born, my prayers for them became more real. Having invested years of prayers before their arrival served to deepen my love for them.

Along this journey of praying for my children and grandchildren, God prompted me to an even grander calling. He told me to pray for my future great-grandchildren and great-great-grandchildren. This was hard to do at first because that reality resides so far in the future. And though it's realistic that I may someday see and hold great-grandchildren, it will only be by God's grace that I live long enough to welcome great-great-grandchildren.

The story doesn't end there, however. Praying for the next four generations of my descendants wasn't enough. God prompted me to pray for the next ten. It was hard to get my mind around this, but I've faithfully prayed for them, as a group, ever since.

Then one day as I prayed, I misspoke. Instead of praying for the next ten generations, I said "twelve" in error. But before I could correct myself, God assured me that twelve is the number I should use going forward.

Interestingly, twelve is a recurring number in the Bible: twelve tribes in the Old Testament and twelve disciples in the New Testament, symbolically connecting the two parts of God's Word. In addition, twelve pops up often in the books of Moses (twelve pillars, twelve stones, twelve loaves of bread, twelve oxen, twelve silver plates, twelve silver bowls, twelve gold dishes, twelve bulls, twelve rams, twelve lambs, twelve goats, and twelve staffs), as well as in the future-focused prophecy of Revelation (twelve stars, twelve gates, twelve angels, twelve foundations, twelve apostles, twelve pearls, and twelve crops of fruit).

And for me, twelve generations.

Beyond twelve, I know that at some point God will up the number to one hundred. That's heady stuff, but when the time comes, I'll embrace the challenge, full of faith that he will answer these prayers for our descendants for hundreds of years to come.

Yet one thing remains. As I pray for our grandchildren and future great-grandchildren and the generations that follow, I continue to pray for our children—all four of them—every day. And I'll never stop.

A Presumptive Question

After our daughter became engaged, friends of mine who didn't know her husband-to-be often asked some curious questions.

Many probed with careful caution. "What do you think?"

"I think it's great!" I always replied.

They'd dig deeper. "But . . . do you *like* him?"

"Most definitely," I declared.

Still, they'd seek confirmation. "So then, you're okay with this?"

"They're a great match, and I couldn't be happier."

The same thing reoccurred when our son popped the question. This time the queries weren't as pointed, yet they came, nonetheless. I suspect some fathers struggle more with getting a son-in-law than they do a daughter-in-law, but I don't know. I'm just guessing. As I said before, I love all four children dearly.

This makes me wonder if some parents, I suspect too many, approach their children's nuptials with apprehension or even disapproval. Yet any opposition will only serve to make their children more intent on getting married.

Why not offer support instead, and give their kids every chance for success? In a culture where many marriages don't last, we must give our children every opportunity possible to beat the odds. This starts by embracing their marriages and their spouses. It continues by praying for them every day.

How Many Kids Do You Have?

People often ask me how many children we have. Sometimes I say two and other times four. It's not that I can't count or don't know. It's that two is the correct answer, but four is the answer I want to give.

We had two children the normal way. We conceived them and brought them into the world. We raised them the best we could. They didn't come with a manual, so we trusted God to make everything work out. After they completed high school, we sent them off to college. They graduated and got married. That's how we got our third and fourth children, through the marriages of our first two. We didn't need to raise child number three or four. We just needed to accept them and love them after their parents had done all the hard work.

I love them all the same. They are my kids, even though I've known the first two twice the time as the other two. We are family, and we're so blessed.

Friday Night Pizza

We're fortunate.

We live close to all four of our children and all our grandchildren. It required moving to make this happen, but it was certainly worth it. If you're curious, we sought the kids' blessing before moving. Though cautiously accepted at first, they soon embraced it. Now we all relish our proximity.

In the process we downsized—though not as much as we had hoped. It was a great move, both literally and figuratively, one worthy of celebration.

Half of our family lives four miles south of us and the other half lives nine miles northeast. It's a quick drive in either direction. We see our family frequently, often multiple times each week.

On Friday nights, the gang meets at our place for pizza. It's the highlight of my week, both emotionally and spiritually. This gives us the opportunity to share a meal and to share life. It's a celebration of family. We have trivial conversations and we have deep discussions. In addition to enjoying their presence, my goal each week is to have significant interaction with each family member. If I'm intentional about it, this usually happens. I'm better because of it, and I pray that they are too.

I'm investing in the next generation. It's my highest calling.

I also realize that this is a season in our lives. As our grandchildren get older, things will pull them in other directions. Pizza with their grandparents may dim in comparison. But while this season lasts, I'm going to enjoy it fully and seek to maximize its value and the impact I can have on my family.

And with God's grace, this season will last a long time. We'll continue to gather for Friday night pizza whenever possible, just as our children did with my parents every Saturday evening.

The legacy lives on.

Easter Communion

Just as Friday night pizza is a weekly tradition, we recently started an annual tradition too: celebrating Communion in our home on Easter. I don't know of anyone who does this, but we do.

You may ask, "We take Communion at church, so why do it at home?" A few churches do Communion weekly, others monthly, and some quarterly. I participate in these events, but I don't feel there's much biblical basis for it.

Here's why.

When Jesus instituted Communion, he did this with his disciples (effectively, his family) in a private setting (someone's home). He did this on the annual Passover celebration. This effectively moved the Old Testament practice of Passover to the New Testament practice of Communion, also known as the Lord's Supper or the Holy Eucharist.

Let's look at the first Passover as Moses instructed God's people. First, it was an annual event. Second, it occurred in people's homes—not a church building. Third, it was with family. And if a family was poor, they celebrated with their neighbors.

So here are the key elements of Passover: annually, at home, with family.

Jesus modeled this when he upgraded Passover to become Communion: annually, at home, with family.

My goal in family Communion is to make it accessible for our grandchildren. This means keep it short, make it significant, and give them something to celebrate. After all, we should celebrate Jesus's once-for-all sacrifice and his victory over death. Yet, at most churches, Communion is a solemn affair suitable for a funeral service and not a resurrection party.

At our house, we use grape juice to make it kid-friendly. My bride bakes some delicious homemade bread. Though a bland flatbread may be more biblical, this isn't something our grandchildren would look forward to eating. I want to see eager smiles on their faces as they sink their teeth into its moist, fluffy goodness.

As we prepare to eat and drink, I say something short, like, "Jesus loves us and died for us so we can live with him forever." As they get older, I may add in a bit more, but not much. They're hungry and ready to dive into Sunday dinner.

And to make the day just a little bit more memorable, Grandma buys a simple gift for each grandchild.

I partake of Communion at church many times throughout the year, but Easter Sunday Communion in my home carries the most meaning.

Peter DeHaan, PhD

Every Family Is Special

As people get to know our family, they eventually learn there's something peculiar about how we communicate. Actually, I suspect more than one thing.

A prime source of amusement is our flexible meaning for the word *box*. In our usage, *box* can refer to anything electronic in nature. Here are some examples:
- The answering machine is a box.
- The garage door opener is a box.
- The VCR is a box.
- The DVD player is a box.
- The DVR is a box.
- Each of our five remotes is a box. (Yes, we need all five, because our universal remote is only semi-universal.)
- And, of course, any storage container is a box.

I want to give full credit to my bride for this wide-ranging application of *box*. Yet, to be sure, I sometimes use it too. Strangely, there's seldom any confusion as to which box she's talking about.

Sometimes, she skillfully uses *box* twice in the same sentence, referencing two different items, as in: "I'm looking for the box to turn on the box." What she means, which I fully comprehend, is, "I'm looking for the remote to turn on the DVR."

Once she used *box* three times in one sentence. "I can't find the box to turn off the box so I can listen to the box." Translation: "I can't find the remote to turn off the TV so I can listen to the answering machine."

Yet with all our boxes, and the confusion that could result, we get along just fine.

However, she does the same thing with the prepositions *he* and *she*. In this instance, she may use *he* multiple times in the same sentence, but referring to different people. I'm not so good at interpreting that one.

For example: He stood up and said he didn't understand what he was thinking. Translation: Nicholas stood up and said that Michael didn't understand what Ian was thinking. Sheesh!

Each person in each family is unique. That's what makes us special. We need to celebrate that. Remember, if we were all the same, life would be boring.

One Kid or Two?

In my family there are a lot of two-children families. My bride and I both came from two-children homes. We have two children ourselves, and they have two children each. Both of our kids' spouses hail from two-children families. Plus, my sister has two children too. So, my mom has two children and four grandchildren. If the trend continues, she will have eight great-grandchildren.

Contrast this with China's one-child policy, which has been in place since 1979. A child born in China today will be the *only* child of two parents and the *only* grandchild of *four* grandparents. If the trend continues, they will eventually be the *only* great-grandchild of *eight* great-grandparents. This child will have no uncles, aunts, cousins, nieces, or nephews.

While this may be an effective means to reduce population growth, it has two negative outcomes.

First, a child born in China will be the only child of two parents and four grandparents. That means that six people are placing their sole generational focus—good or bad—on that one child. They'll tend to spoil their *only* child and grandchild. This places tremendous pressure on that boy or girl to do well, succeed, get married, and have their one child. This puts a huge burden on one kid. Besides this, all these overly-indulged, only-child kids will be the center of their family's attention. They risk becoming narcissistic.

Second, this one child in China will be the only grandchild to care for four aging grandparents and, later, the only child to care for two aging parents. They'll have no siblings or cousins to share these duties. Again, that's a lot of responsibility to place on one kid.

In societies with no procreation limits, parents rightly make their own decisions on the number of children they will have, be it ten, two, or even none. This is as it should be. But when a government forces its entire society to limit themselves to one child, the ramifications are significant.

Regardless of the size of our families and the number of children we have, may we thank God for those he has given us. May we cherish them and seek to influence them for the kingdom of God.

2.

Holidays

Bring the fattened calf and kill it. Let's have a feast and celebrate (Luke 15:23).

A holiday is a great excuse to celebrate with family. These can be for fun or for spiritual reasons, but let's make them for both.

I Heart You Day

My wife and I aren't the romantic types. I'm not sure if I'm just bad at planning and execution or if gifts and surprises aren't all that important to her. Nevertheless, I do put forth some effort from time to time, with full knowledge that every romantic overture I've ever made has failed . . . miserably. It started with our first Valentine's Day when we were barely engaged. I still shudder at how badly that one went.

Even so, we sometimes go out for dinner on Valentine's Day or a day in reasonable proximity. One of us may have a gift for the other, or not. That's okay. No one's keeping score. Well, at least, I'm not.

One January, my bride asked for a new printer. Teasingly, I suggested it could be a Valentine's Day present. She agreed—seriously, she did—with the stipulation that it included spare ink cartridges. So a plan emerged—a good one.

I ordered the printer and hooked it up the weekend before. It was an arduous task. Everything that could go wrong went wrong, but that's a story for a different time.

On Valentine's Day morning, I presented her with a box of her favorite chocolates. Unfortunately, she still had some left from her birthday. Could it be she didn't like them all that well anymore?

That evening I made a special dinner—chicken stir-fry with sweet and sour sauce. I planned a candlelight dinner, but it wasn't dark enough for candles and she opted for the more convenient option, called electric lights, with a dimmer switch. We finished with the Valentine cupcakes she had made that morning.

Waiting at her plate were her ink cartridges. She was pleased—at least I think so. Or was she just amused?

Then we watched a rom-com. I'm okay with chick flicks, but I gave this movie only three stars out of five. I think she was even less impressed.

To wrap up our romantic evening, I retreated to write while she watched TV. It was a good Valentine's Day—at least I think so.

Thank you, God, for my wife.

Celebrating St Patrick's Day

Let's play word association. I say "St. Patrick" and you might say "March 17," "shamrock," "three-leaf clovers," "Ireland," or "leprechaun." To be cute, you might even answer with an Irish brogue. You may salivate over imbibing green-hued adult beverages. And, of course, you'll think green.

Just like Christmas and Easter, we've lost the original meaning of St. Patrick's Day over time, altered by rampant commercialization. While most people are aware of the origin of Christmas and Easter, albeit faintly, few people know about the work and person of the man we call Patrick.

Let's clear up some misconceptions. First, Patrick wasn't a Saint (that is, Rome didn't canonize him). He wasn't Irish. He was English. And the whole thing about his ridding Ireland of snakes is a myth.

Patrick went to Ireland as a Christian missionary. Actually, he went twice. The first time unwillingly, as a slave, the second time willingly, as a missionary.

As a Christian missionary, he targeted those in power. Their conversions had a ripple effect throughout the entire population. For thirty years, he traveled Ireland, promoted Christianity, and started churches and monasteries.

Patrick had a huge impact on Ireland for God.

History says he died on March 17, 461 (yes, a long, long time ago). This marks the day we commemorate his life of spiritual service and God-honoring accomplishments—by celebrating the myth that surrounds him and the traditions we made up.

What's Good about Good Friday?

Some Christians celebrate Jesus as their suffering Savior on Good Friday. Others celebrate him as their risen Savior on Easter. Which is he?

Both.

Jesus is both a suffering Savior and a risen Savior. That's why we need to celebrate both Good Friday and Easter.

Without his resurrection on Easter, Good Friday wouldn't matter so much. It would be sacrifice without victory. Yet without Jesus's suffering on Good Friday, Easter couldn't happen. We need both.

Good Friday is good from the standpoint that it was the sacrifice to end all sacrifices. His one-time sacrifice eliminated the need for an annual sacrifice for our sins. Good Friday is good because, through Jesus's death in our place, he reconciled us into a right relationship with his Father, who I call Papa. Good Friday is good because God accomplished his mission through his Son, his *only* Son.

But Good Friday wasn't so good for Jesus. He endured physical suffering greater than I can ever comprehend as the soldiers abused him and tortured him before executing him on the cross, the Roman Empire's cruel instrument of death.

Jesus also endured spiritual suffering beyond my ability to fathom. In his sacrificial death, he carried with him the burden of all my sins, all your sins, and all the sins of the world. He died for our mistakes so that we could live forever, free from the weight of our errors, which he has forgiven—eternally so.

Thank you, Jesus.

Resurrection Sunday (aka Easter)

Jesus is the focal point of the Christian faith. The physical part of his story begins on Christmas and ends thirty-three years later, on Easter. But in a spiritual sense, Easter is the beginning. Jesus's story arc goes like this: Jesus is born. He dies as the ultimate sacrifice for our sins. He rises from the dead to prove his authority over death. Jesus returns to heaven and sends the Holy Spirit to his followers. His church is born.

We get five major spiritual celebrations from this: Christmas, Good Friday, Resurrection Sunday, which we call Easter, Ascension Day, and Pentecost. How awesome is that?

No one knows where the name *Easter* came from. It's not in the Bible. (Christmas isn't in the Bible either, but at least we can easily see the name *Christ* in the word *Christmas*. There is no such obvious connection with Easter.) Many who attempt to explain the origin of the name *Easter* tie it to various pagan practices. That's why I prefer a more descriptive and less ambiguous name for Easter: Resurrection Sunday.

Easter carries with it the secular traditions of cute bunny rabbits that somehow lay multicolored eggs.

Talk about whacked. Resurrection Sunday has no confusing baggage. It's about the resurrection—the resurrection of Jesus. Even though many churches observe Easter and don't mention Resurrection Sunday, I view Easter as a secular holiday and Resurrection Sunday as a spiritual celebration.

One of our newer family traditions for Easter—I mean Resurrection Sunday—is celebrating Communion as a family in our home. (If this offends you, remember that Passover—from which we get the Lord's Supper—occurred with family in homes.)

Following Communion, we have a family feast. This is where another of our traditions comes in: empty tomb rolls.

You can find the recipe online, but here is the essential information: wrap dough around a marshmallow and coat it with butter, cinnamon, and sugar. As it bakes, the marshmallow melts. This leaves the finished product with a hollow center. When you bite into the roll, it's as if we peer inside Jesus's tomb. But it's empty. He's not there. He has risen. He has risen, indeed!

Happy Thanksgiving!

I'm thankful for family and friends.

I'm thankful for food, clothing, and shelter.

Mostly, I'm thankful for Jesus.

Everything else is a bonus, and I'm thankful for that too.

If you celebrate Thanksgiving in your country, may you have a wonderful day. And if you don't celebrate an official Thanksgiving holiday, may you take a moment to thank God for all he's done for you.

Our Christmas

To celebrate Jesus's birthday, my bride starts preparing around the middle of August, looking for specific sales and making gifts. Even so, we're usually among the last to put up the Christmas decorations. While many stores have been decorated for Christmas since Halloween (or earlier) and neighbors string their lights before the first snow, we often lag in this area.

But at last, our tree goes up and the living room furniture shuffles to accommodate it. The fireplace mantle receives a yuletide makeover, and multiple manger scenes adorn our home.

Baking begins in earnest as the Queen of Desserts works her magic. I eat too much and gain a few pounds. The Christmas season is here.

Most years our Christmas celebrations begin the Saturday before Christmas with one side of our family. They continue Christmas Eve with the other side. And they conclude Christmas morning with our children and grandchildren. By 10 a.m. everyone has left for more family celebrations of their own. But my wife and I have finished our Christmas gatherings.

We spend a quiet afternoon, often going to the theater to watch a movie.

I'm always shocked at all the people there on Christmas Day. I wonder if they're like us, having completed their celebrations early. Or might they have no family to celebrate with, so they go to the movies instead? Or does Christmas mean nothing more to them than a day off from work, with the movie theater being their best option for something to do?

I hope this isn't your situation. I pray that your Christmas is a joyous time, spent with family and friends—along with time to relax.

Happy birthday, Jesus!

Your Christmas

My Christmas wish for everyone is a joyous time of celebration with family and friends. May your home overflow with laughter and love.

May your table overflow with food and delight.

May you give gifts well and receive them even better. For it is, truly, better to give than to receive.

And may you take a moment to thank the One whose birthday we celebrate.

As you spend this season with family and friends, may your celebrations be joyous and your time together uplifting.

Their Christmas

Regardless of the needs in your life, remember others whose needs are even greater or whose burdens may be heavier. Despite our circumstances, God has blessed us indeed.

Yet people have needs, often critical ones. If you can donate money, now is the time to do so. If a monetary gift isn't possible, give your time; there's always a need for volunteers. Of course, we can give both our time and our money.

With each Christmas holiday season, do what you can to help those in need, but remember that they don't need help just at Christmas but year around. As we do this, we'll keep the Christmas spirit—that is, the love of Jesus—alive in us and in those around us throughout the year.

I pray you'll enjoy Christmas—and help others do the same.

Happy New Year!

The practice of staying up late to greet the New Year always seemed strange to me. Even though I stayed up until midnight when I was a teen, the idea of forgoing sleep for a sixty-second countdown to the New Year perplexed me.

As I grew older, I became less of a conformist and more practical. Now I turn in at my normal time and get up at my normal time. The New Year arrives just fine without me.

Welcoming the New Year is also a time when people make New Year's resolutions. I've never figured that out either. Common resolutions include losing weight, drinking less alcohol, or quitting smoking. Others are promises to save money, be more generous, or find a better job. Then there are the vows to return to school, get out of a bad relationship, or be kinder.

All too often, these well-intentioned resolutions have a short life. The problem is that people set themselves up for failure.

Let's assume that in September I step on the scale and decide I'll make a New Year's resolution to lose weight. Since this is a future goal, I don't need to worry about it now. I can continue eating what I've always eaten. I know that in four months, I'll need to change my eating habits and get serious about weight loss, but for now, no worries.

This gives me four months to further ingrain bad eating habits and gain more weight. Additionally, knowing that in the future I'll need to be more careful in what I eat emboldens me to eat poorly now—while I still have the chance. This only exacerbates the problem now and results in more weight to lose later.

A better approach is to start weight loss efforts as soon as we notice a problem. In this example, it would be in September, not January.

That's why I don't make New Year's resolutions. As soon as I realize I need to change something, I set about doing so right away—before things get worse and while I have the best chance for success.

If you've made New Year's resolutions this year, I pray for your success in keeping them. However, if you stumbled, don't give up or defer another attempt until next January 1. Just forgive yourself for not following through, start over, and ask God for help.

Have a Happy Normal Day

With Christmas and New Year's behind us, it's time to get back to normal.

It's refreshing to have time off from work for the holidays, wonderful to celebrate with family, and enjoyable to feast upon holiday foods. However, it's also good to return to a regular routine—for things to get back to normal.

For as wonderful as the holidays are, I like normal too. Normal is how I keep disciplined and remain focused. Normal allows me to get important things done.

Sometimes the transition from holiday mode to normal mode takes time. I move from holiday to nearly normal and then on to completely normal. I think this is the same for others as well.

May our holidays be great and our normal days even better. May we see God in them all.

3.

Seasons Change

> *See! The winter is past; the rains are over and gone. Flowers appear on the earth; the season of singing has come, the cooing of doves is heard in our land. The fig tree forms its early fruit; the blossoming vines spread their fragrance (Song of Solomon 2:11–13).*

I celebrate the changing seasons, though I appreciate some more than others. I see God's hand at work through them all as I celebrate his creation. Join me on my journey through the seasons.

Four Seasons

Where I live, we experience four definite seasons. We have summer sunshine and winter snow. We have a springtime warmup and a fall cooldown.

In the summer, the typical high temperatures are in the mid-80s F (27°C), with the heat index a few degrees higher. Yet we occasionally break 100°F (38°C), with heat indexes upwards of 110°F (43°C)—or more. We enjoy the sunshine and have about fifteen hours of daylight at its peak. My typical attire is shorts, T-shirt, and tennis shoes. My yard work includes watering the grass, weeding, and mowing the lawn.

In the winter we have snow—several months of it—and temperatures typically below freezing, with extremes going below 0°F (-18°C) and wind chills dipping below -20°F (-29°C) or sometimes worse. For this season I wear long pants, wool socks, a shirt, and a sweatshirt—and that's inside. My outdoor responsibilities are clearing the walks and driveway of snow and ice. This means shoveling and snow blowing, sometimes more than once a day.

Both fall and spring weather hovers between these two extremes. What I wear and what I do ramps up and ramps down as the seasons change. In fall there are leaves to rake, and in spring there are flowers to plant.

I enjoy this variety of seasons. I need this variety in my life. Without the changing seasons, I'm sure I'd quickly end up stuck in a rut.

Yet, to be sure, I appreciate some of God's seasons more than others.

Summertime

For myself, along with many others in the United States, summer effectively begins on Memorial Day and ends on Labor Day. Yet for those of us in the Northern Hemisphere, summer officially starts around June 21—give or take a day—and lasts for three months.

I love summer.

With warm temperatures and lots of daylight, I spend more time outside, enjoying God's creation. I celebrate this amazing world he made for us to live in. There are also more activities to relish in the summer. We can walk in parks, enjoy a picnic outing, or go to the beach.

My yard work peaks in the summer, but that's okay. I water the lawn when we don't get enough rain. I apply fertilizer to keep the grass green and control weeds. (I see fighting weeds as a spiritual issue. Check out Genesis 3:17–18.) I mow the lawn every four or five days because I water and fertilize it. Yet most times, I appreciate this excuse to get outside, claim some exercise, and enjoy the place God has given me to live.

I mentioned two US holidays that occur in the summer: Memorial Day and Labor Day. In between we have Independence Day, which we often call "the Fourth," because it falls on July 4. Each of these three holidays offers a break from our normal routine. We cease work, relax, and spend time with family. We may take in a parade and savor grilled foods. These are all part of our summertime celebrations.

Thank you, God, for giving us summer.

So Long, Summer

At the beginning of each summer, I create a mental list of things I want to accomplish, some fun, a few relating to home improvement, and others for my yard. Each year, summer ends before I complete my list.

By this time, kids have already returned to their classrooms. At the same time, we kick off our fall programs at church. Yet these programs apply to all of us, whether we have kids in school or not.

The weather, of course, begins another transition on our migration from summer to fall. I put away my shorts and T-shirts for another season and pull out my jeans and long-sleeve shirts. I don't need to mow the lawn as often. The leaves turn colors, morphing from their normal emerald green into vibrant reds, bright oranges, and playful yellows. Thank you, Papa, for the beauty of your creation. Then they turn brown and fall to the ground. This gives me leaves to rake.

With summer over, I review my to-do list. Some of the remaining items move to my non-summer list, others wait for next year, and the remaining I discard on the junk heap of good intentions, mercifully forgotten.

So long, summer. Hello, fall.

Fall Has Fallen

Fall means I won't water the lawn for the rest of the year, and mowing the grass will occur much less often. In fall we have cooler temperatures, serving as a nice reprieve from the summer heat. We no longer concern ourselves so much with applying sunscreen when we go out. And we pull clothes out of our closets that we haven't worn in months. It's like getting a new wardrobe without spending any money. How amazing is that?

Fall also provides one last opportunity to wrap up all the projects I had planned for the summer but didn't yet get to, thinking I can put things off until tomorrow or next week because the weather will be just as nice then. Then the press of changing seasons provides the motivation for me to make a final push to complete my to-do list.

The amount of daylight shrinks by a couple of minutes each day. It's a reminder to make the most of the sun while it still shines. More than once I will complete an evening session of mowing lawn with the outdoor lights turned on so I can see what I'm doing. On these days, squeezing in mowing the grass between supper and sunset is an increasing challenge.

You'd think I'd embrace fall because it means less yard work. While this is true, one thing I dislike about fall is the knowledge that winter will soon follow.

But right now, I need not dwell on it—and enjoy fall while it lasts.

Thank you, God, for giving us fall.

Winter Is Here

The winter solstice (usually near December 21) marks the first official day of winter, but it normally feels like it's been winter for a month and a half, with three more months—or more—to go.

On my list of favorite seasons, winter ranks fourth.

It's discouraging to already be tired of snow on the first day of winter, but there's an upside. December 21 also marks the day with the least amount of sunlight, so for the next six months the amount of light will slowly increase each day. On the winter solstice sunrise occurs around 8:10 a.m. and sunset around 5:15 p.m. That's about nine hours of light for the day—and fifteen hours of dark. However, by the summer solstice (around June 21), it will be just the opposite.

Despite my aversion to snow, it's nice to enjoy a white Christmas.

Merry Christmas!

After Christmas is New Year's and then the long slog to spring. I figure if I can make it through January, the worst is behind me, and I'm on the home stretch.

For all I complain about winter, cold, and snow, I praise God for it. Winter helps me appreciate the other three seasons even more.

Lord, thank you for winter.

Spring Has Sprung

This past weekend a glorious thing happened. I noticed a couple of daffodils poking through the cold ground. They haven't produced flowers the past few years, so after transplanting and fertilizing them last fall, I expect them to bloom this year. (It might be the last chance I give them.) Even so, it's refreshing to see a hint of life in an otherwise dreary landscape. I see a few tulips too.

I also spotted a robin. This fills me with glee. Truly. The returning robins, which are a migratory fowl, mean spring will soon be here. The males come back first to stake out a territory, and the females follow when the temperatures climb a bit higher. Yes, warmer weather will soon be here.

Spring is my favorite season.

Summer is grand, fall is pleasant, and winter is something to survive. However, spring is the most splendid time of the year.

Spring is when the cold desolation of winter fades, the dirty snow melts, and plants push forth green, restarting for another year. Spring is an especially spiritual time for me, signaling reinvigorated life and a fresh beginning, a new birth of sorts.

Jesus had a new life in spring too. After dying for us to reconcile us with Papa, Jesus was buried and then overcame death to live again. Each spring reminds me of this and what he did for us.

Thank you, Jesus!

Soon I'll see which plants survived the harshness of the winter months. I expect most will. Next, the grass will green, and with it, a slew of yard work will follow. But that's okay. It's spring, and I want to get outside and do something other than shiver. Being outside working in the sunshine is a welcome prospect after a season of being cooped up inside.

The landscape in my yard will turn from winter drab into springtime brilliance. Throughout the spring and summer, I'll enjoy dashes of color as various plants share their glory, following the unique schedule God gave them.

Thank you, Papa, for giving us spring.

Celebrate the Seasons

As I said, spring is my favorite time of the year. Spring signals new life, fresh beginnings, and personal rejuvenation.

Summer comes in as a close second, with warm days and a less hectic schedule. I so enjoy summer. It's almost as grand as spring.

Then comes fall, which weather-wise is an okay time of the year. But I don't like what fall foreshadows: winter.

Winter is the season I tolerate. I grit my teeth and endure it. I know, I must develop a more positive attitude about this season of cold and snow, but it's hard for me to do, and it gets harder every year.

Yet without winter, I wouldn't appreciate spring, summer, and fall as much. I thank God for them all—even winter. The seasons bless me with variety and something new to embrace every three months. Without the changing seasons, I'd surely grow bored.

God knows what I need, and he gives it to me.

Thank you, Heavenly Father.

4.

❖

God's Creation

And what does the Lord require of you? To act justly and to love mercy and to walk humbly with your God (Micah 6:8).

We tend to make our relationship with God complicated. Yet Micah tells us God wants only three things from us. He wants us to act with justice, embrace mercy, and walk with him.

It's easiest for me to walk with him when I walk in his creation.

I'm in awe of God's creation—his attention to detail, its interdependence, and the uniqueness of each element he made. As a good steward of what God has given me, I seek to take care of it. I don't want to disregard God's gift of nature, and I certainly don't want to misuse it.

I celebrate God's creation when I spend time in it and as I care for it.

Let's Take a Walk

I love to walk in God's nature. I do this every chance I get. It's a spiritual time for me—more so than the rest of my life. When I immerse myself in God's creation, I feel closer to my Creator. I worship him through his amazing work. I praise him, and we talk.

Occasionally I go on a spiritual retreat to a rustic setting in the middle of nowhere. There's not even cell phone coverage, which is a welcome bit of freedom. After dinner, I take to the trails. I walk about a mile, covering only a portion of the many paths in the area. It's August, so it's hot and humid. If I slow my pace, the bugs quickly attack. So out of self-preservation, I maintain a brisk pace. Intentionally quick is how I normally walk, but it's not an ideal tempo for contemplation and prayer.

Even so, I'm drawn to consider God's wondrous creation—and what humans are doing to it. Some say the earth is fragile and we must take care of it, even to the point of great cost and substantial struggle. Others claim God's creation is resilient and adaptable, able to counteract whatever people do to it.

On the trail in God's woods, I realize both perspectives are right, and both are wrong. God did make the earth resilient and adaptable, able to deal with anything that nature can throw at it. Humans, however, are a different story.

We've advanced to a point where our consumption, our greed, and our disregard for his creation are indeed threatening it. We must be careful with the habitat God has gifted us. We must be good stewards and wise caretakers. Furthermore, we must take steps to reverse the damage we've already done.

Yet there's no need to overreact. God's earth can take care of itself if only we give it a chance.

An Unexpected Encounter

As I continue my walk, I notice deer tracks on the path, first just one set and then a second. Not expecting to witness any wildlife, I'm quite surprised when I round a bend and spot a deer some thirty feet away. She doesn't run. For quite some time we just stare at each other. The deer has no fear of me. I imagine that's what it was like with Adam in Eden, and what it will be again when God restores all things. I have an unexplained urge to talk to her, but that would be irrational, so I remain quiet.

I want to wait in this sacred moment, but the insect portion of God's creation wants to taste my blood, so I begin to move, albeit slowly. The deer stands still as I gingerly advance. I expect my approach will spook her and she'll flee. She doesn't. When I close to within fifteen feet, she saunters off the trail, showing no sign of fear or running away. Without a care, she meanders off into the woods. I circle around and five minutes later find her in about the same place. She spies me watching her but nonchalantly lowers her head and returns to sniffing the ground before her.

I cover about a third of the trails that evening, praying as I walk. My prayers are not a monologue to God or for God, but a holy communion with God. We connect on a spiritual plane, a supernatural level. It isn't so much of words, but it's a presence, a being, an existent reality.

We don't need words. In fact, they would only get in the way. Yes, there are times of articulated interaction, albeit silently, but mostly it's a time of spiritual meditation, of basking in the growing awareness of his essence all around me. So it was when God revealed his truth to me about his creation and humankind's stewardship of it. So it was when this deer showed up and God reached out to embrace me.

Why Recycle When You Can Refuse?

Each week someone delivered a free paper to our home. Each week I walked it from the paper-box to the trash can. When Dad was alive, he would recycle these papers for me, but with shorter hours at the recycling center and higher gas prices, we often wondered if his efforts were worth it. Now, without Dad's help, these papers become instant garbage.

I had received this paper for years. But I never wanted it, never read it, or never used it (except as a fire starter or to use when painting).

One day I'd had enough.

Instead of feeling guilty about not recycling this paper, I decided to avoid the issue by not receiving it in the first place. I took down my paper-box. However, the resourceful carrier merely put the paper in a different place. Next, I called the publisher. To my shock, they cheerfully canceled my subscription. Refusing the paper was much easier than recycling could ever be.

Encouraged by this, I next tackled the free magazines I receive that I don't want or read. Most of them just started showing up—and kept showing up. I canceled more than a dozen. Some were easy to stop, and others took a bit more work. But I gladly did so as my part to help the environment. Next, I tackled catalogs. This was easy. I went to catalogchoice.org to stop receiving them.

A related effort was dealing with the unsolicited offers I received in the mail, especially for credit cards. I tried to contact each company to stop their mailings. Sometimes that worked. But if I couldn't reach them, then I took their offer, wrote "Not interested. Please remove me from your mailing list" on it, and returned it in their prepaid envelope. If they ignored me, the next time I returned their envelope empty. My bride doesn't like my passive-aggressive behavior, but it's a way to get back at these unresponsive companies and generate a little more money for the post office in the process. (Since the US Postal Service loses billions of dollars every year, they can use all the revenue they can get.)

Another area of refusal—I've been doing this for years—is bags for the merchandise I buy. Why do people think that one item needs to go into a bag? Clerks are shocked when I decline their bags. And they're stunned when I remove my purchase from the bag, leaving the unused bag for the next customer. I do the same for two or three items, though I recommend using a bag for more than six. I learned that lesson the hard way—the result wasn't good. Sometimes we need a bag.

Refusing trumps recycling every time. It may not be much, but if everyone does a little, it can add up to a lot.

Save a Tree

A mailed statement, one of the last ones I received, claimed that "for every 13 people who go paperless, one tree can be saved." Really? What does that mean?

It's an ambiguous statistic that doesn't make sense. What does make sense is going paperless when it's sensible to do so.

Yet going paperless and then printing out the paperless statement gains little. So, if you need a hard copy, don't go paperless. However, it's great to receive statements electronically, store them electronically, and destroy them electronically when no longer needed. No more shredding.

I'm all for saving God's trees and doing so whenever it's practical. Yet sometimes the effort to save a couple of pieces of paper is too time-consuming and frustrating, so I'll pass. Remember, planting a tree will replace the one I used, but the time lost in trying to save the tree is gone forever.

We must keep our efforts to save a tree, as with all things, in balance. Sometimes the effort doesn't justify the results.

Going Paperless

Most companies have stopped sending customers their invoices and statements through the mail. Instead, they use email. They do this to save the expense of printing and mailing paper documents. Their customers benefit by receiving their information faster. They can also file it digitally, without the need to waste paper. However, I wonder how many people print the invoice or statement anyway. (One person in my household seems to print documents that don't warrant it, but she will remain nameless.)

I both love and hate this practice of going paperless.

I love it when companies email my invoice as an attachment. It's easy to access, view, and file. It saves time and doesn't consume any natural resources.

However, I hate it when they email a notice telling me my invoice or statement is available online. Then I need to go to their website, login—often a multistep process—navigate to the appropriate page, find the desired document, download it, open it, and then save it.

The process is easier if I click on the link provided in their email, but I don't do that because of the danger of falling victim to a phishing scam.

But when companies force us to go paperless, it isn't a customer-focused practice. If a business is truly interested in serving their customers, they would offer options: paperless or paper. It's the right thing to do.

Still, I'm glad for the opportunity not to waste paper and to do my part to save a tree. Yes, trees are renewable resources, but we shouldn't misuse them.

More Than Walking

Though I can best appreciate God's creation and draw closer to him when I walk in the beauty of what he has made, I can also celebrate him in other ways as well. This includes gardening, observing wildlife, and even watching the weather.

Let's not forget that God has made an amazing place for us to live. May we always celebrate his creation and never dismiss it.

5.

Gardening

The Lord God took the man and put him in the Garden of Eden to work it and take care of it (Genesis 2:15).

One of the reasons I so enjoy spring and summer is the chance it gives me to get outside and enjoy God's creation. This includes the part of his creation that surrounds the house he has blessed us with. I celebrate this spot of land because he made it and gave it to me to care for.

Joy fills me as I work in his creation. I praise him for his amazing goodness.

Pursuing Green

Over the years my attitude toward lawns has changed.

I must have spent too many hours mowing the lawn as a teen because when my bride and I bought our first home, I didn't care what the grass looked like. It could be weedy and brown, but if it looked trimmed from the road, it was all good.

After a while, my attitude changed, perhaps because brown grass isn't much fun to see or to walk on. My new goal became to have a yard that was both mowed *and* green. I didn't care if it was full of weeds, providing they were green weeds. This required me to water the lawn during dry spells, but that was okay if it produced the verdant yard I desired.

This phase didn't last long, however. I soon became dissatisfied with neatly mowed green weeds. I wanted a weed-free lawn. This required me to apply fertilizer and weed killer four times a year. But to get the most out of the product, I needed to water more.

Overall, I'm pleased with the results—and the yard looks great. Alas, with fertilizer and more watering comes more mowing. As it turns out, pursuing a well-trimmed, vibrant-green, weed-free lawn requires time and effort. But the enjoyment I get from having a lush, green lawn is worth it—most of the time. Caring for my lawn is an act of worship.

I know how to have a lousy-looking lawn. Been there, done that. And I've figured out what it takes to have a good-looking lawn. But I wonder if the ideal lawn is partway in between: one that looks okay but doesn't take much time to maintain.

Unfortunately, I don't know how to do that.

April Showers Bring May Flowers

Each spring my yard comes alive with color. In addition to the greening of the grass (winter-brown gets old), I enjoy flowers of all colors. First up is my flowering crabapple tree. It bursts into lush, white flowers every spring, which lasts two or three weeks.

Next is the periwinkle (also called Vinca minor or myrtle). This groundcover produces light blue flowers in the spring. It continues flowering throughout the summer, but it isn't as profuse as in the spring.

I also have several varieties of phlox, which flowers in the spring, lasting three or four weeks. They haven't been doing well the last few years since nearby trees now cast more shade than the plants like. One variety is candy stripe phlox, billed as "extremely rare" by the nursery—so rare that of the fifteen plants I bought, only four were, in fact, candy stripe. The rest were white or various shades of pink. Still, they provide beautiful splashes of color in the springtime.

Interspersed with them is dragon's blood sedum, which has lush foliage and scarlet flowers in late summer to fall. Given that this area now has more shade than it once did, I expect the sedum to eventually overtake the phlox.

I also have snow on the mountain, a handsome plant with variegated white-and-light-green leaves. My high school agricultural teacher, however, didn't appreciate this plant so much. He called it goutweed. He had no taste.

Other plants in my landscape include ferns, pink bleeding heart, and crown vetch. They give me something interesting to admire throughout the growing season. From early spring to mid-fall, there's always something blooming in my yard to appreciate. However, the colorful flowers and blossoms are most prevalent in the spring. That's why we need those April showers, to bring May flowers, as well as June, July, August, and September flowers.

Thank you, God, for the rain needed to make your plants grow. Their beauty praises you throughout the year.

Time to Move the Sprinklers

Although my goal is to find a balance between my lawn's appearance and the amount of work required, I have yet to discover how to achieve that. Part of the issue is watering.

The use of water isn't a concern. Irrigating a lawn doesn't consume water. It merely takes water from the earth and redistributes it—mostly back to the ground, with a bit evaporating to eventually join rain-producing clouds. Though it requires some electricity to pump the water, that's not an issue for me.

My concern is the act of watering. For most people this isn't a problem. Just program the irrigation system and forget it. Not so with me. I go old school, dragging hoses around and carefully pointing sprinklers so that my lawn receives its needed hydration in exactly the right places.

Sometimes this is a hassle, and I wonder why I do it. However, by hand moving sprinklers I can direct water to where it's most needed: extra attention to the dry spots and a quicker pass on the shaded areas. You can't do that with an in-ground system. Part of the lawn will always be overwatered, while a few areas will inevitably be stressed.

Overall, I enjoy this task of watering. It gives me short, periodic breaks from work, allows me to go outside, and provides satisfaction. I often find that when I'm in "watering mode" (that is, moving sprinklers every thirty minutes) I work more efficiently. This is because I work with greater intention between my trips outside to move hoses.

I set an alarm on my computer for thirty minutes. When it goes off, I tell it to snooze for thirty more and head outside to reposition the sprinklers. It's fun for a few days, but when a dry spell lasts too long, it gets old. But at least the grass is green, and I get to spend some time outside in God's creation.

A Micro Garden

"Can we have a vegetable garden?"

My bride's question caught me off guard. We've not had one for twenty-five years, not since we moved to this house.

"No!" End of discussion. I wasn't about to dig up the lawn for a vegetable garden. Besides, our rapidly growing maple trees provided too much shade for there to be any good garden space.

At our former home, we did have a garden. This was partly because the house came with one, but also because anything we could do to stretch our food budget was a good thing.

The garden took a lot of work, which fell mostly to me. The toil required for a bountiful garden wasn't a surprise. As a child I'd witnessed the many hours my dad spent on his, but then, he enjoyed it. I do not. It is fun to plant seeds and watch for the miracle of green popping through the dirt. Later it's fun to pick the produce, but everything in between is a chore, which I'm glad to skip.

My total lack of support didn't dissuade my wife, however. A few days later she announced she'd planted beans in her flower garden, a small spot under our picture window. She normally plants annuals there. This year she diverted the space for her micro garden.

About a week later, I saw the beginnings of plants, a straight row of delicate tiny sprouts. They weren't beans.

She beamed. "Oh, I planted beets too."

Later the beans popped up, and the rabbits quickly found them, gnawing most plants down to the ground.

An internet site suggested human hair would serve as an effective bunny-be-gone treatment. That night my bride gave me a haircut and added the trimmings to her micro garden. I wasn't sure how long the scent would remain on my hair to repel rabbits, but it was a couple of weeks, giving my hair time to grow enough to produce the next crop of bunny repellent.

In another section, around the corner from the beans, she planted tomatoes. They fared a bit better, but not much.

That fall I cleaned out the micro garden, and next spring my wife planted flowers—to my great relief.

The Last Yard Work for the Season

Our yard boasts ten maple trees. Naturally, they grow bigger each year. This means they make more leaves. That's more shade for me to enjoy in the summer, but also more leaves to deal with in the fall. Their falling foliage covers most of my yard, often several inches thick.

Fortunately, leaf removal is the one task I hire out. It's the only yard work I don't do myself. Ten healthy, growing maple trees produce too many leaves for me to deal with. So, I called my leaf service, and in a couple of hours, a team of three had the leaves corralled into a pile alongside the road. Then a day later, another company came with a giant leaf vacuum, sucked them up, and hauled them away.

It's nice to see green grass again—at least until it snows.

I've finished my yard work for another year. Now I'll enjoy a short, God-given break until I switch to snow removal mode.

Then We Moved

I worked hard to make a nice yard to frame our house, with verdant grass and splashes of color throughout the growing season.

Then we moved to be closer to our kids.

Now I get to repeat the process with the new house. But rather than figure this out myself, I'll tap the expertise of a landscaper to offer professional advice and avoid my trial-and-error approach to creating an attractive setting for our home and a tribute to my Maker.

This time I expect better results in half the time. This means more joy sooner.

6.

❖

Weather

Then the Lord spoke to Job out of the storm (Job 40:6).

Earth's weather can present a powerful force: tornadoes, monsoons, and hurricanes. It produces a variety of storms, including, rain, sleet, hail, and snow. Sometimes our weather is less severe, be it too much rain or not enough, too hot or too cold, and too humid or too dry.

Though we seldom appreciate our weather extremes, they are a function of the world God created for us. And as he did with Job, God can speak to us through it.

Are we listening?

It's That Time of Year

Each fall I brace myself for the first snowfall. This is, in part, because it signals what is to come, but also because it takes folks a while to adjust their driving habits to snowy conditions.

First, we need to allow more time to get where we want to go. That's key. Slower speeds are critical, with more time needed to accelerate and much more time required to stop.

With the first snow of the year, I always warn anyone who will listen to drive carefully and keep a wary eye out for those who aren't.

My preference is that the first snow would arrive on Christmas Eve and then melt on January second, after which spring would begin. So far that's not happened, and it never will. Instead, we'll have several months of snow. But just because it's inevitable doesn't mean I have to like it.

For the record, I allow myself to complain about the winter, which is my least favorite time of year. But as a tradeoff, I try never to complain about the other three seasons because, from my perspective, they're so much better in comparison—regardless of the weather they throw at us.

Lake-Effect Snow

When people call me during the winter, they often ask about the weather, usually about the amount of snow, but sometimes it's the temperature. I suspect they hope my winter weather is worse than theirs—and for most of them, it is.

Living east of Lake Michigan, this Great Lake strongly affects our weather. First, the lake has a moderating effect on our temperature. Summer winds cool as they cross this massive body of water, while the lake warms the winter air. These are good things, and I'm thankful for them.

The bad part is that as the air moves across Lake Michigan, it also picks up moisture. First, this produces clouds. Michigan has far fewer sunny days than does Wisconsin, situated on the windward side of the lake. (I know. We lived there for a time.) When these clouds float over the land, they cool, producing precipitation: snow in the winter months and rain in the others. If you've ever heard about lake-effect snow, this is it. Living about forty-five miles from Lake Michigan guarantees us receiving lake-effect snow.

Regardless of how much snow we receive, each winter I mark off the days until spring—and hope I can hold out till then.

Let It Snow!

One Christmas, friends from Southern California visited. Although my buddy grew up in Michigan, complete with its snowy winters, his wife and their three sons only knew of California weather. As such, they hoped to experience snow during their Christmastime visit. They weren't disappointed.

With only mild embarrassment, they admitted to becoming distracted by the awe-inspiring beauty of the snow in the mall parking lot. Taking pictures of the fluffy white precipitation soon turned into a spontaneous snowball fight. People stared, but my friends didn't care. The snow was too glorious, and their joy abounded. (It's inconceivable that I would ever use *joy* and *snow* in the same sentence, but I just did.)

They hoped for more snow—and the opportunity to take more pictures. They got their wish.

As a winter-jaded Michigander, I approach the snow season with a little less enthusiasm each year. Yes, I want snow, but it doesn't need to last for three or four months. Regardless, I do occasionally thank God for snow because it helps me better appreciate the other three seasons.

Unseasonably Warm

Late one spring it got a tad hot, surpassing the 100°F (38°C) mark at my house. Though it's not unheard of to hit 100 degrees at some point during the summer, those highs usually occur in August, not in June. It was over 100 degrees at noon. When I checked again at 3:00 p.m., it remained at 100 degrees. By 5:00 p.m., it had cooled down to a more reasonable 96°F (36°C).

On the news that morning, the weather service issued an ozone warning alert for my county. Among other things, I'm not supposed to mow the lawn.

These ozone alerts always perplex me.

I could have mowed the lawn yesterday. I expect it will be okay to mow the lawn tomorrow. But mowing the lawn today is *bad* for the environment. This implies that mowing the day before or the day after would have been environmentally okay.

I'd like to point out that to wait and mow the lawn tomorrow will take longer, thereby causing *more* ozone-damaging pollution. Regardless, my grass hasn't stopped growing and needs my attention. I guess my lawn is unaware of this ozone issue.

I'm left wondering how I can balance caring for creation with using common sense.

Weathering the Storm

After a night of high winds, I went out the next morning to check for damage. I spotted three birds' nests the gusty gale had ripped from my trees. Although saddened by the loss of habitat for my animal friends, most of the nests had been empty at the time. Only one poor creature didn't survive.

However, one nest smartly survived the bluster. It sat snugly secured above a crook in my downspout, safely beneath the protective overhang of my home's eaves. This was a good thing, too, as it was home to three baby robins. I noticed them that morning during my inspection of the storm's damage. But later that day, one had already left the nest.

That evening, I spooked another. With instinct overcoming him, and a mighty squawk and sputter, he took to flight. I witnessed his first successful flapping of his wings. His parents were aghast, making quite a fuss in the process. One flew close to where the fledgling had landed, and the other served as an irritating distraction, offering a cacophony of sound and sight.

By the next day, the youngest sibling had likewise left home.

The nest sat empty, but ready for a new family. Robins often have two broods a year, so Mom and Dad could return for a repeat performance later this summer.

The Comings and Goings of Toads

Where do toads come from?

I pondered this question after a massive deluge as I peered out my basement egress window into the window well. Sitting there as happy as could be were two toads. Being different sizes and colors, I assumed they weren't related, yet they both turned up together.

What was interesting was that they weren't there prior to the rain and they weren't there a few days later. Even more perplexing is that the window well is about four feet deep with nearly vertical sides, so although they could have jumped in, they certainly couldn't have jumped out. Gravel fills the bottom of the window well. Under the gravel is a wire mesh. Moles occasionally bypass the mesh, so I suppose the toads could have as well, but the toads are a lot fatter, making the task more challenging. Besides, I don't envision them as tunneling animals.

I frequently see toads around my house in the moist dirt as I weed flowerbeds, so I know they're nearby, but when it rains, they become much more apparent.

Then there are frogs. The closest water—their normal habitat—is a small stream about a quarter mile away. Yet when it rains, they, too, show up at my house. Afterward, they disappear.

I went online for answers, but my simple query about where toads come from opened a Pandora's Box of related questions but left me with the unanswered question: How did the toads get out of my window well? Though I don't know, God does.

This Is for the Birds

After a much-needed rain, I noticed a robin's nest had fallen from my crabapple tree. I mourned the three unhatched eggs lying on the ground. Their parents were gone, and it was too late for me to do anything about it. Even if I had discovered the eggs right away, the chance of keeping them warm enough to hatch would have been a long shot, not to mention feeding them once they hatched. Then I would face the challenge of reintroducing them to the wild.

Interestingly, the nest was intact. It just hadn't been properly anchored to the tree. I could see where it had been attached, and though it was at a crook in the tree, it wasn't an optimal one. Additionally, since robins often lay eggs twice a year, these parents will need to build a second nest if they intend to try again.

As a nature lover, I derive great joy observing the life of animals. Although death is a normal part of nature, it's a part I prefer to overlook. Yes, I know about natural selection and the survival of the fittest. Unfortunately, these babies never had a chance because their parents hadn't built a secure home. It's a small consolation to know that their deaths will keep this particular trait from continuing in the gene pool.

The lesson in this is to be careful when choosing what foundation we build our lives on. Make sure it is a firm one. Rarely in the United States does this have literal life-and-death ramifications, but in other parts of the world it does, primarily the third-world parts. In first-world situations, the wrong foundation could include living in a bad neighborhood, sending kids to an ineffective school, starting a business without a plan or enough capital, investing in a shaky opportunity, and so forth.

Just as with building bird nests, it's important that we find the right foundation and carefully build upon it. The consequences of not doing so can be dire.

In matters of faith, which carry eternal ramifications, Jesus is the only foundation that matters.

7.

❖

Wildlife

Now the Lord God had formed out of the ground all the wild animals and all the birds in the sky. He brought them to the man to see what he would name them; and whatever the man called each living creature, that was its name (Genesis 2:19).

Animals are part of God's amazing creation. As we enjoy the animals he made, we worship him as their Creator. My wife and I live in a subdivision in a decreasingly rural setting, which limits wild creatures to decidedly smaller and less wild varieties. Yet here are some of God's animals I enjoy from my backyard.

Woodpecker Wars

I like woodpeckers. They're part of God's amazing creation. I admire their colorful beauty and stately appearance. I'm amazed at their peculiar characteristic of using their beaks as a boring tool to find food or make a shelter.

However, when I learned that woodpeckers had taken an interest in my neighbor's house, I immediately checked mine. When I saw the results of their efforts on my home, my appreciation of woodpeckers dropped a bit.

They had been hard at work on the shutters on the north side of our house. Fortunately, it was only the shutters. They left our cedar siding untouched.

My bride went online and quickly learned the following:

- It's usually just one or two woodpeckers that attack a house, not a flock of them, despite what the evidence may suggest.
- They have a variety of motivations for their pecking habit: looking for food, establishing a nest, or trying to attract a mate.
- No one solution to get rid of them comes with a guarantee. There's only a list of possibilities that might work, which may hinge on their motivation for pecking.

- Anything that hurts or kills a woodpecker—or disturbs their nests—is against the law. They live a legally protected life. (Not that I would want to harm them, but recalling the tenacity and speed of their work, courtesy of the old Woody Woodpecker cartoons, I imagined things quickly escalating out of control.)

As a first step, I filled the holes with plastic wood. Once cured, it was much harder than cedar and not at all attractive to woodpecker beaks, though I did see evidence of a couple of beak marks before the plastic had hardened. I'm sure that surprised my feathered friends.

This solution solved the problem—for a few days. Though they never returned to the north side of my house, they moved their focus to the shutters on the south side, which I filled twice.

I made a daily walk around my home's perimeter, searching for the telltale signs of a woodpecker at work. So far, so good.

Oh, Deer!

In my yard I regularly celebrate seeing gophers, rabbits, and squirrels. There are many moles too, but I seldom spot them. I find only the mounds of dirt they make in my yard. Birds abound during the non-snowy months. It's rare for me to look outside and not catch a glimpse of at least one in my backyard. I have toads, the occasional frog, and newts that appear every spring in a window well.

A neighbor tangled with a skunk one night, but that was years ago. I pray I never repeat his experience. Although deer live nearby, I've never seen one in our subdivision. That is, until a Saturday morning one spring.

Around noon, a blur of brown rushed past the window. Two deer, only a few feet from our deck, darted across our backyard. They were in a full-on panic.

As my bride went for her camera, the deer scurried to our neighbor's, but stopped short. Something spooked them. They made a U-turn, then scooted between our houses and sped toward the front. My wife, camera in hand, headed to the back of our house as I moved to the front. I tried to update her on their ever-changing location, but my hurried words fell short.

The deer leaped through our front yard and across the street. My wife reached our front door just as they ducked behind another neighbor's house. As she looked out the front door, I was at a different window, watching them disappear behind the house next to that neighbor.

In a flash, they were gone. She never did see them, so she must take my word for it. I did see two deer, dear. Really, I did.

The Birds

A side effect of moving sprinklers every thirty minutes is enjoying the activity of baby birds in my lawn—more so than I would have guessed possible on our small subdivision plot of land.

Usually, when I see a baby bird in the grass, it seems abandoned, left to fend for itself. Twice I witnessed baby birds who, although out of their nests, were still under Mom and Dad's care, as the parents provided a steady supply of food. One bird seemed to grow by the hour, and after a couple of days, he had become mature enough to fly away. All he left was a pile of poop where he had sat in the grass.

Sometimes the babies are either too young to be afraid of me or too petrified to move. All they do is watch me as I walk around. I've gotten within a couple of feet of them, and they still don't move. They just blink. One perched on my hose. Unable to coax him off, I gently pulled the hose, but he hung on tightly while I moved it several feet.

Another time, a baby wren hopped around looking for food. A parent followed. When junior flew off, so did his parental unit.

What amazes me most is when I witness a baby bird's first flight. These are a bit older and bigger than the ones that just watch me.

As I approach these birds, they panic. They hop a bit or flap their wings, but they don't fly. As I get closer, their movement becomes more frantic, and they jump higher and flap furiously. Still, flight eludes them. As I move even closer, they put forth more effort. This time they might rise a couple of inches off the ground. In their next effort, they fly a few fluttering feet. Then farther, and eventually they successfully fly to a nearby tree. As a result of their fear of me, these panicked birds learn to fly.

It's so amazing to witness.

The Power of Panic

These birds' panicked motivation reminded me of when I was much younger. A friend and I played in a sandpit next door. My little dog jumped in to join the fun. When my friend and I grew bored, we climbed out, but my dog couldn't.

The bank of the pit was too high for him to jump and too steep to climb. His repeated efforts ended in failure. No amount of coaxing or encouragement worked. I jumped in to help, but he was too heavy for me to lift, and each attempt failed.

I decided a stepladder might help. I told my loyal dog that we'd be right back and hightailed it to get a ladder. I had hurried only a few steps along my journey when my faithful dog showed up by my side.

Overjoyed, I bent down and gave him a grateful hug. Apparently, if he could see me, he wasn't too concerned, but once I faded from view, his panic of my abandoning him produced enough adrenaline for him to escape.

For both baby birds and my dog, panic helped these animals do something they wouldn't have otherwise done. The same is true with people. When we face the direst of situations, we can do the most extraordinary things.

Birdbrain Behavior

The numerous maple trees and blue spruce in our yard provide ample and ideal nesting sites for several varieties of birds.

Most noticeable are robins. I know this because they throw a fit if I get anywhere close to their nests. Sometimes they fly straight at me at full speed, veering off at the last moment. I'm not sure how close they come to making contact, but it seems it's within inches. One time, a particularly aggressive bird was so unrelenting in its attacks that I gave up working near its nest.

We also have mourning doves. I have no idea how many nests are in our yard because their behavior is the opposite of robins. When potential danger approaches, the mourning doves in the nest freeze, doing nothing to alert a predator to their presence. Once, while doing some minor tree trimming, I reached for a small branch to lop off and noticed a mourning dove quietly perched in her nest, which was only two feet away. She stared at me but didn't move, looking like a statue. I watched for several seconds before I convinced myself she was alive.

I decided to trim that tree later.

I checked on her from time to time. She was always in the same pose, but no matter from which direction I approached, her head always faced my way. I don't know how long it takes mourning dove eggs to hatch, but she's been waiting a long time. I hope the outcome is positive.

For those who think all birds are the same, they're not. Robins deal with predators much differently than mourning doves. God made them different, just like he made you and me different. Isn't variety great?

Feeding Rabbits

I have a burning bush next to my house. I love its vibrant red leaves in the fall, a visual allusion to God's encounter with Moses in the desert through a burning bush—one really on fire yet not consumed.

Rabbits love the burning bush too. This burning bush has become a favorite hangout for them. It's not that I see them there, but I've noticed where they bed down for the night. I also spy where they've nibbled on the bush as well as the droppings they produce after they digest their nibbles. They leave piles of evidence. Although unsightly, it provides a nice supply of natural fertilizer for the bush in the spring.

It doesn't surprise me that bunnies eat the burning bush. This has been common over the years. In a harsh winter, they've eaten an entire small bush. They must consider the tender twigs a preferred delicacy. Fortunately, the larger, more aged branches are either too big or not tasty enough, so my bush is safe.

Though they eat the bottom branches, it's the top that needs a trim. I've been trying to figure out a way to get the rabbits to eat the top of the bush rather than the bottom. This would save me some extra work in the spring. But lacking four feet of snow—to cover all but the bush's upper reaches—it looks like I'll be the one doing the trimming.

Raccoons in the Neighborhood

I never saw a raccoon near my house until one day, as dawn peaked forth. Setting the sprinklers for the first watering of the day while not fully awake, I shuffled around my house, looked ahead, and saw a raccoon lumber across my yard. He waddled in my direction. I froze. What should I do?

Do I yell to scare him off? Chase him away? Ignore him?

In my early morning stupor, visions of a comedy/horror skit flooded my mind. I imagined him rearing up on his hind legs and charging. With lightning quickness, he would attack, mouth foaming and eyes ablaze. Before I could react, he would leap into the air, lunge at my chest, and pin me to the ground. Then he would . . .

I shuddered, shaking my over-active, God-given imagination from my foggy mind. Though not logical, I shook with fear.

I clapped once to get his attention. He looked up with a start. He, too, seemed in a predawn stupor. To my relief, he made a U-turn and padded out of sight. He wasn't full-grown, but with quite a tummy on him, he appeared well-fed.

I recalled my neighbor catching two adult raccoons in her live animal trap earlier that spring. I wondered if those were my raccoon's folks. The trap still sat in her yard, ready for a third, but this lad was too clever. If he was an orphan, he was doing okay, avoiding capture, and finding plenty to eat.

Mr. Raccoon, I hope you have a long and happy life. Just do it in someone else's yard.

The Return of the Woodpeckers

Though it looked as if I had taken care of the woodpecker problem at my house, I was wrong. It happens.

After a couple of weeks of woodpecker-free days, they returned. This time I heard their incessant *rat-a-tat-tat* on the side of my house.

They had already caused significant damage to several other houses in our neighborhood. I didn't want mine added to the list. The law said I couldn't hurt them, but it said nothing about giving them a good scare. I tore out of my front door and rounded the corner. I waved my hands, jumped up and down, and screamed like a madman.

They took one look at my foaming mouth and flew to a nearby tree. I charged them, and they flew away.

Confident I had accomplished my objective (and relieved no one had seen my impression of a raving maniac), I went back inside and returned to work.

An hour later the *rat-a-tat-tat* returned. I reprised my former role as a deranged lunatic. Once again, they flew away to safer environs.

They didn't come back that day, but tried again the next. I soon learned that I didn't need to act completely crazy to get them to leave. Waving one arm and shouting, "Get out of here," was enough to send them elsewhere.

This continued for a week. When I grew tired of this game, I tried a shortcut. I learned I could stay inside and still shoo them away. All I needed to do was pound a couple of times on the wall inside my house near where they were working and yell, "Leave!" That was enough to do the trick.

After a couple of weeks, they left for good. Thankfully, I can now appreciate them from a distance and not worry about them making holes in my house.

Animal Rescue

Our basement has two egress windows, and over the years many animals have stranded themselves in the window wells. I've rescued many from these unintended traps—one rabbit and a couple of birds. Usually, I tie a string to a pail, lower it into the window well, and tip it on its side. A bit of coaxing, along with a dose of patience, does the trick to get the trapped critter into the bucket so I can raise them up and set them free.

Other unfortunate critters include frogs and toads. Each spring, newts (salamanders) have found themselves entrapped. Though I assume the newts hatch there, the other animals must fall or jump in. They all depend on me to get them out, removing them by hand.

That leaves the moles. These buggers tunnel up from the bottom. Never mind that it is four feet deep and I lined the bottom with wire mesh and covered it with gravel. They still manage to burrow their way in. As soon as they exit their tunnel, the gravel caves in, and they can't dig back out. In their panicked attempts for freedom, they work themselves into a frenzy and quickly die. It's not a pleasant end. Unfortunately, I usually don't find them until it's too late.

One time, however, I spotted one right away. I vowed its story would have a different ending. He moved too fast to catch by hand, and the pail technique didn't work—with the opening being round, he would always escape. I needed something with a rectangular opening. I taped a square plastic container to a long board. After my seventh try, I caught him. I pulled him out of the window well and released him into my yard. Now he is free to dig up more of my lawn.

Though the thought irritates me, I'm glad I could prolong his life rather than find his dead body in my window well.

Squirrelly Behavior

The squirrel population around our house is on the increase. One of their favorite pastimes is gathering nuts from my neighbor's trees and relocating them to my yard. They've done this for years with acorns, resulting in my having to pull up tiny oak saplings each spring.

Now they've added hickory nuts to their repertoire, as my bare feet frequently encounter whole nuts and empty shell fragments in my lawn. Though they try to bury their treasures, my sod is too thick to allow them much success.

These squirrels are increasingly comfortable around humans, too, no longer scurrying away as I approach. Last week I saw one squirrel furiously pawing at my grass, attempting to dig a hole at the base of a maple tree. He was not successful.

I approached him to scare him off. He stopped digging, gave me a long look—not fearful, but amused. I think he was grinning at me.

As I inched closer, he rolled over on his back. At first I thought it was a posture of submission, as some animals do. Then he shimmied from side to side, rubbing his back over the hole he was trying to dig, feet flailing in the air with unabashed jubilation. I'm sure he was laughing at me, daring me to come closer.

When I got about ten feet away, he scampered around the tree trunk, poking his head out to watch my approach.

I circled the tree and so did he. He scurried up several feet so we could look each other in the eye. I think he enjoyed this game as much as I did.

We played hide-and-seek for a while, but then I couldn't find him. Eventually looking up, I spied him perched on a branch, peering down on me from a safe distance.

I told him to stop digging in my lawn.

I think we reached an understanding.

Crazy Rabbits

A lot of rabbits are in the area where I live. Though common, they're not a daily sight, but then I don't spend my time gazing out my window either. I'm supposed to be working. When I see one, it's always alone, which I find a bit sad.

But one day I saw two hanging out, hopping, and playing tag. Then a third one appeared. One jumped left, the other scurried right, while the third scampered in a circle. On the smaller side, they could be siblings from this year's litter.

Then, to my delight, a fourth one bounced into view. A bit larger and more deliberate in movement, I surmised this to be their mom. They didn't seem to have a care, content to dance around in my backyard.

Those cwazy wabbits.

I watched them for quite a while, admiring their zest for life in the afternoon sun.

I'm glad I took the time to watch them frolic. It was good to slow down and marvel at God's gift to us.

What do you do to slow down?

The Woodpeckers Strike Back

The woodpeckers terrorized our neighborhood and hit five houses hard. They caused thousands of dollars of damage. I was the only one who escaped costly repairs. This is because I was the only one who worked at home and could shoo them away. (One of the many benefits of working from home.)

Despite my desire to keep my house free of woodpecker-created holes, I did take time to admire their beauty. They are a smart-looking bird, with dashes of bright colors.

Though I never want to hurt an animal, and I have the highest regard for its habitat, I wonder if there is a practical limit we should place on our efforts to protect them. Houses aren't woodpeckers' natural habitat, so how do we balance our right to protect our property with their freedom to build nests anywhere they want?

I don't have an answer, but I do know that animal species have been dying out since God created our world because they couldn't adapt to changing conditions. This is sad, but what's sadder is when people, instead of natural events, cause the changes that result in their extinction.

Where Do Frogs Come From?

One night while mowing my lawn, I saw three frogs in my yard. Though I would occasionally see frogs right after a rain or around damp groundcover, I never noticed them in dry grass. In twenty-four years of living there and mowing my lawn, this was a first.

Where did the frogs come from? I know the biological answer and the evolutionary answer and the creation answer, but those are the wrong answers to my question. I want to know why this trio of amphibians suddenly showed up in my yard.

- There is no water nearby.
- We are not in a low spot.
- My lawn is not even damp.
- Given the drought earlier this summer, the water table is surely lower than normal.

Where did these frogs come from?

I did an online search and got tired of reading before I found an answer. Maybe a biologist will someday answer this perplexing question for me, but until then I'll just have to wonder. Or I can wait until I get to heaven and asked the lead biologist who created the frogs in the first place.

A Lesson on Compassion

I learned something disconcerting about myself.

Once, when moving sprinklers, I was horrified to see three too-young baby birds on the ground. They couldn't fly, and one couldn't even hop. When I approached them, they opened their mouths in the hope of receiving some needed food. I had compassion, but I froze with indecision. A myriad of thoughts rushed through my mind:

- I don't know what to do.
- They're going to die anyway.
- I'm too busy.
- What if they carry disease?
- Shouldn't I let nature take its course?

I checked on them with each move of the sprinklers. My compassion for them remained, and I tried to justify my inaction. A couple of times I saw an adult bird on the ground near them. I convinced myself that their parents were tending to them. Yet each time I approached, the babies turned my way and opened their mouths, clearly wanting to eat.

By the next day, the weakest of the three wasn't looking too good, and he later died. Would I likewise witness his siblings' demise?

On the third day, one of them was clinging to the side of a tree and later he was gone. I never saw him again and assume he flew away.

On the fourth day, the remaining bird hopped with a bit more vigor. For the first time he instinctively flapped his wings. An hour later, he too was gone.

I should be happy that two out of the three made it, but I wonder if I should have tried to help their weaker brother.

What I do know is that compassion without action is worthless.

Then We Moved

I mentioned that about the time I got our landscape in order, we moved to be closer to our kids and I had to start all over again setting my new yard in order. Though our present home shares many similarities with the house we moved from, the wildlife I see from my office window at our new home is surprisingly different.

Of course, we have birds, squirrels, rabbits, and toads, but not as many as we had at the previous home. Since a bit of water is nearby, we have lots more frogs, as well as turtles and animals I can only appreciate from a distance: snakes. Yes, they're small and harmless, but I don't like snakes—unless they're behind a glass enclosure at the zoo.

We have muskrats, which are fun to watch as they graze in my lawn, but their underground activity makes a mess of my yard. Fortunately, they've moved on. Though they no longer give me the joy of watching them, I still have the occasional agony of twisting my ankle when I step into a hole they left for me.

I'm also treated to an occasional sighting of a mallard duck or blue heron. And though they never stop by, I do see the flight and hear the prehistoric-sounding caw of the sandhill crane. I also occasionally see wild turkeys and am more apt to spot deer. I even had a repeat experience of watching two panicked deer dart around our neighborhood as they frantically searched for their way back to the woods. They made it.

God, thank you for all the animals you made and for giving me so many opportunities to admire them and worship you through them.

8.

❖

Health

> *Jesus answered them, "It is not the healthy who need a doctor, but the sick. I have not come to call the righteous, but sinners to repentance" (Luke 5:31–32).*

This is a curious verse about health.

On the surface, it's about the importance of physical health. If we're healthy, we don't need a doctor.

However, Jesus is addressing spiritual health. Jesus came to heal and to save. He came for us. We're the sick ones in this verse, not the Pharisees. Strange.

Our physical health intertwines with our spiritual health and vice versa. May we desire spiritual health even more than we desire physical health.

Thank you, Jesus, for the physical and spiritual healing you provide.

The Effects of the Flu

I'll spare you the details, but I recently had the flu. Here's what I learned:

- I don't appreciate my health—until I lose it for a time.
- Having the flu is a tough way to lose weight (but I do know that I could never be bulimic. I don't have the stomach for it.)
- I've regained half of my flu-generated weight loss, which I expected, but I won't be disappointed if the rest of those pounds never return.
- When I'm sick, I want someone to take care of me, but my bride wants to keep her distance. She claims I'm a big baby. She might be right.

Being sick reminds me to thank God for my health when I get better—and to even thank him when I'm still sick.

Do You Lie to Your Doctor?

At work I received a shocking press release. In part it said, "It's an open secret in healthcare communities: patients lie."

The reasons are many. Some lie because they don't want to admit unhealthy behaviors to their doctors. For others, by not voicing a concern, patients subconsciously deny its existence. Still others make their own determinations as to what's important and what's not, lying to keep from revealing what they deem irrelevant.

Yet I think I understand this. I've made casual comments to doctors, and the next thing I know they want to schedule me for a series of tests unrelated to my visit, or they prescribe a medicine for a minor issue, but the drug's side effects are worse than my minor ailment.

Doctors have also quizzed about trivialities, which they verbally regurgitate visit after visit, long after I've forgotten them, as in: "Are you still suffering from blurred vision?"

"That was three years ago," I respond, "and I haven't accidentally poked myself in the eye since then."

Too often doctors only half listen. Once they hear a certain keyword, they tune out the details that surround it. They leap to a diagnosis or treatment for a problem that isn't there or doesn't matter.

Sometimes when we lie to doctors, it's simply to keep them from reaching a wrong conclusion and subjecting us to needless pain and expense.

Yes, I've lied to my doctors. Though lying is a sin, I don't feel too bad about this one.

The Christmas Five

I gain five pounds—or more—over each Christmas holiday. It's all my wife's fault. Really, it is. A few days before Christmas, she, the Queen of Desserts, goes on a baking spree, producing a bodacious bevy of delectable desserts that would put a bakery to shame.

Ahh! So much to enjoy. So little time. What am I to do?

First, I attack the Rice Krispies Treats. Soft and tasty and good for you too. Since they're made of cereal, and cereal is good for you, the Treats are good for you. I don't want to say that I eat them all—so I won't.

Pecan bars, a personal favorite, catch my eye next. They are so rich, however, that I invoke a self-imposed, two-a-day limit.

Then the sugar cookies, puppy chow, chocolate chip cookies, macaroon kiss cookies, cheese fudge, gingerbread cookies, and a birthday cake for Jesus.

This makes sense since Jesus is the reason for Christmas. It sounds a bit corny, but we sometimes sing Happy Birthday to him. At some point, a light-hearted discussion ensues. I usually start it off by saying that somewhere in the Bible it mentions Jesus likes yellow cake with lemon frosting. My bride assures me his preference is chocolate.

Anyway, until I eat all the desserts, there's no chance I'll lose the five pounds. Gingerbread cookies are my least favorite, but until I properly deal with them, there is little chance of my losing my Christmas five.

Until then, happy snacking!

Though I blame my wife for my holiday weight gain, it's misplaced. She doesn't force me to open my mouth and enjoy all her desserts. It's my lack of self-control that's at fault. It's a spiritual issue.

Time Lag

We've all heard about jet lag, that messed-up, disconcerting thing that happens to our bodies after flying across time zones. I've heard that each time zone crossed equates to one day of recovery. Personally, I think that may be generous.

A similar disorder happens to me each time we switch from *normal* (Standard) time to Daylight Saving Time (DST) and vice versa. I call this phenomenon *time lag*.

Each March in the United States—as well as in many other countries—we set our clocks forward one hour as we *spring* forward into spring and DST. We stay in this mode for seven months, and then we *fall* back to Standard Time.

Though some people think DST saves time, it doesn't. All it does is shift the clock setting to give the illusion of more sunlight. Nope. It shifts time but does not save it. If we want to be honest, let's call this Daylight Shifting Time.

The result is that time is neither created nor lost. Instead, it's merely the perception by some that they gain time through this temporal sleight of hand. This means that every man, woman, and child in the countries that shift their time will realize an annual time savings of exactly zero.

About seventy countries currently observe DST, though they may follow a different schedule than in the United States. Each time I adjust clocks for DST, I wonder about the cost of switching to and from DST—and the amount of time it *takes*, not *saves*.

First, doing some projections based on my personal clock-setting experiences, I calculate that people in the United States spend about 150,000 hours adjusting clocks each fall and spring. For businesses, this has a direct labor cost. To determine the full expense, however, factor in all the devices inadvertently broken while trying to set them.

Next, consider all the commitments, appointments, and flights missed because people show up at the wrong time. In the fall, it's not so bad, as we arrive early and end up waiting for an hour. In the spring, it's a killer because we arrive an hour late.

Altogether, this adds up to a huge cost, burden, and time waster—all for the delusion that we are saving time.

I've never been a fan of our twice-annual time change, in and out of DST. I want to pick one time and stick with it. This is in part because of the hassle of resetting clocks but also because it takes my body up to a week to adjust. During this time, I'm tired, have trouble focusing, and lack motivation.

If it takes me a week to adjust in the spring and again in the fall, that's two weeks per year adapting to or from DST, which is about 4 percent of the year—and 4 percent of my life.

I'd just as soon forget the whole DST thing. If we did, we'd have more time and be healthier too, because we wouldn't be tired from switching our clocks.

Find Time to Slow Down?

Don't feel bad that you missed my birthday this year. I have everything I need and most of what I want. So it's all good!

It's the time spent with family and friends that is the most significant and best part of a birthday.

I always receive birthday cards, including those from service providers, such as insurance agents and financial advisors. I was first amused and then taken aback by the generic message in one such card that read:

"Wishing you time to slow down and enjoy your special day."

What does this say about the pace at which we move today? Is being too busy so common that a wish to slow down has become a universal sentiment? I hope not, but I fear it has.

This isn't to imply that I don't need to sometimes slow down, because at times I do. Sometimes my workload overwhelms me. Sometimes I get frustrated by the commitments I've thoughtlessly made. And sometimes I say, "I'm too busy," because I am.

It took me a while to learn that I have the freedom to say no. I now often say no to *good* things so that I may have time for the *best* things. When I consistently do this, I don't need to slow down to enjoy the day. I'm already moving at the right pace, which allows me to enjoy most every day that comes along.

Regardless of the speed of your day, I hope you enjoy yours.

The Stress of Time

I used to fixate over knowing what time it was. I was a slave to the clock. Glancing at my wristwatch became a compulsion, an obsession. And the more concerned I became about time, the more often I looked. This is the dark side of time management.

As I planned my daily activities, I did so under the assumption that each task would proceed ideally and without problems. I constantly checked my watch to see if I was on track or falling behind. But since real-world realities would eventually overtake my unrealistic schedule projections, I often ended up feeling pressed and stressed.

As a result of checking the clock so frequently, I could tell someone what time it was—plus or minus a few minutes—without looking.

One day I'd had enough. I quit—cold turkey. I took off my watch for good.

I made this decision after being on a delayed flight. I was concerned about making my connection and nervously peered at my watch every few seconds. Yes, every few seconds. How absurd! No matter how often I checked, I could not affect the outcome. I would either make the connection or miss it. So why subject myself to the added stress of worrying about the time?

I still want to arrive at places on time, and I don't like to make others wait for me, but beyond that, time isn't the stress factor in my life that it once was. I wish that for everyone.

What time is it?

Who cares?

That sums it up.

My Routine

If this chapter veers a bit toward the tedious for you, please stick with me. There's a purpose to it.

I thrive on having routines. My routines give me structure. They allow me to be productive while keeping God at the center of all that I do.

I begin each morning with prayer before I venture into my day. With raised arms, in a physical display of worship, I give my day to God. I dare not get out of bed until I do. I ask him to walk through the day with me, seek his favor, and ask for his blessing. Specifically, I request Holy Spirit insight for my writing. As I review my plans for the day, I ask him to go with me. I refuse to get up until I feel he and I are on the same page. It's folly to do otherwise.

Then I bound into my day. Well, sometimes it's more of a shuffle.

After shaving, I exercise. It's on my stair stepper that I pray for our children and future generations. Prayers continue while hanging upside down on my inversion table, requesting blessings for those close to me and for my writing. Then it's on to my exercise bike. As I peddle, I read my Bible. I've done this all my adult life. My mind is so conditioned to read God's Word from the seat of my bike, that this is where my best Bible reading takes place. I end with a prayer for my bride.

Then it's to my office. I make relevant notes about what I've learned from the Bible or do additional study on my computer. Then I check email to see what awaits me, specifically if any messages are from my assistant, who starts her day much earlier than I.

With email dispatched and distractions removed, I spend an hour or so on a writing project. Then it's off to breakfast and then a shower. Often, I receive Holy Spirit insight for something to write. It's amazing what inspiration comes as the soothing warmth of water covers my body. And I must capture this revelation as soon as possible.

I spend the rest of my morning writing or editing one of my books.

After lunch, I go for a walk as I listen to podcasts. This refocuses me, preparing me for the afternoon. As my mind engages with the recording, my body relaxes and my spirit celebrates the world God has placed me in.

I spend the afternoon working on my publishing business or writing for my clients. I do this until supper.

After dinner, I may have a project around the house or some non-work-related task. To wind down I (and sometimes *we*) watch a movie or TV show. This may last until bedtime, but if not, I wrap up my day by reading.

I crawl into bed and conclude my day with prayer. I ask God to bless my sleep and provide the rest I need. Usually I'm sleeping by the time I finish this part of my prayer, but if not, I'll continue in my time with God by moving into my version of an Examen. In this, I review the highs and lows of the day. I thank God for his blessings. And if I'm still awake I thank him for helping me through my struggles or confess my shortcomings or ask him to help me do better next time. Rarely do I get this far. Usually he blesses me with sleep well before this point.

This is my Monday through Friday schedule, with a slight variation on Thursday: I do a twenty-four-hour fast (most) every week. The purpose of the fast is to honor God, being more purposeful about walking with him throughout my day. Sometimes I spend what would have been lunchtime praying and listening to him.

On Saturday I alter my weekday practices a bit more. I skip my morning exercise. Having a day off from my mini workout is the only way I can embrace the practice for the other six days of the week. By design I do no writing on Saturday. I focus my day on larger projects for work and home.

On Sunday, after my morning exercise, I write my blog posts for the week. Since this writing addresses biblical spirituality, it's a fitting way to focus my mind on my Sabbath practices. Weather permitting, I walk to church, this time without earbuds. My intent is to center on God and what he has planned for us at church.

My bride drives and meets me there. After church, we often have lunch with family followed by an afternoon of rest. There may also be other activities with family and friends. I do no work and don't write (except for my blog posts). If I handle my Sabbath properly, I'm primed for another week.

The intention of how I treat my days and weeks may seem extreme to some. It may appear too controlling, even constraining. Yet, I need my routines for structure. I thrive on them. They free me.

Though this is my ideal plan, some days don't work out so well, but most do. And the details of my schedule subtly morph over time as I tweak them to help me better engage with family, work, and God. Although the specifics may shift, the overall intent doesn't.

With my practices for each day, I normally accomplish much while keeping God at the center of most all that I do. And with the rhythm of each week, I move through my days with purpose, again with a focus on God.

For me, my routines keep me anchored in the spirituality of everyday life.

9.

❖

Work

> *So I saw that there is nothing better for a person than to enjoy their work, because that is their lot. For who can bring them to see what will happen after them? (Ecclesiastes 3:22).*

In the book of Ecclesiastes, Solomon shares the angst of his soul as he probes life's oldest question: what is the meaning and purpose of life? After all his meanderings, Solomon eventually gets to a cogent conclusion, but along the way, we don't want to miss his one-liner about the importance of enjoying work.

My prayer for you is that you will have work that you enjoy.

I Love My Job

I love my job. Really, I do. Not only does it provide me with income, but it also affords me fulfilling work. I see my work, all facets of it, as a way for me to help others. How amazing is that?

However, I didn't always love my job. I remember a season of life when I would come home from work, and the first thing I would say to my bride was, "I hate my job." This went on for a couple of years.

You may wonder why I persisted.

The sad truth was that I didn't believe I had any other options. Finding another job in my profession would require moving. Been there, done that. I didn't want to separate our children from their grandparents again, but to find another job without moving would mean going into a different line of work and accepting a cut in pay. Neither solution was acceptable, so I stayed where I was, working a job that paid well but robbed me of joy.

As the sole income provider for my family, I had to put my wife and children first. I needed to take care of them. My needs came second. Yet this job was slowly killing me, both literally and figuratively.

However, something changed. Some of the change occurred in the job, but most of it took place in me.

First, I had put too much pressure on myself. I had a career path taking me where I wanted to go, but it was a long road with an unsure end. If everything panned out as I hoped, I would reach my objective about the same time I would hit retirement age. This made no sense. I discarded the occupational future I hoped for as being unrealistic and perhaps not even attainable.

Next, I stopped caring as much about work. In truth, I cared too much. I had an ownership attitude even though I didn't own the business. You might say I was working hard for the man. Not that I disliked working hard, but I was making too many sacrifices to benefit someone else.

Third, as I stopped pushing to reach an uncertain future, I began to look at life more short-term: Not next year but this week. Not this year but today. I found more to look forward to in the day-to-day. When I focused on the present, I discovered tasks to anticipate and moments to relish. Gradually, joy reemerged.

As I made these three adjustments, my attitude for my job changed. My joy for work re-emerged.

That was decades ago, and since that time I've changed careers—two or three times. This allowed me the freedom to explore, to experiment, and to discover the place where I fit; to find a place I liked, earn an income, and enjoy fulfilling work.

I'm now a full-time writer, at least in the way most writers define it. This doesn't mean I spend forty hours a week writing books. Though I do spend fifteen to twenty hours a week doing exactly that, I also spend time as a commercial freelance writer, writing for other people. In addition, I work as a periodical publisher and editor. Presently, these last two endeavors pay the bills so I can pursue my passion for writing books, which I hope will one day pay the bills.

Each of these three areas helps other people.

The books I write help readers on their spiritual journeys. I pray that my words bring them closer to God. My freelance work helps businesses grow their companies and communicate better with their clients and prospects. And the periodicals I publish help readers through the information I provide while offering businesses an advertising option.

I love helping others, and I love my job.

Thank you, Papa, for giving me the ability and willingness to work. Thank you, Holy Spirit, for guiding me to work that's the right fit for me. And thank you, Jesus, for the opportunity to tell others about you and encourage them on their faith journeys.

Pursuing a Forty-Hour Workweek

After I adjusted my attitude toward work and began to again enjoy it, this gave me the opportunity to consider more carefully what I was doing. Though as a teen I had a few jobs as a laborer, much of my work as an adult has been white-collar. I have the physical capability and the mental stamina to work fifty to fifty-five hours a week, every week. Exceeding that many hours wears me down. Though I can work extra hours for one week, pushing myself for more than that leads to a serious misalignment.

In considering how many hours I worked, I realized that when my workload surpassed my fifty-five-hours-a-week threshold, I subconsciously began to self-regulate what I did. Out of necessity, I would eliminate less critical functions, streamline other duties, and be more open to delegate tasks.

This pattern repeated many times.

If I could successfully hold myself to a fifty-five-hour workweek, why not use the same principles to move me to a forty-hour workweek? Though it took deliberate effort, I soon scaled back my work to accomplish all essential tasks within forty-five hours a week. Though I could occasionally get down to forty, it was rare, albeit enjoyable. However, a forty-five-hour workweek became both doable and sustainable.

Where am I now?

That's a great question. I suspect I'm bouncing between forty-five and fifty hours a week. I'm okay with that because I enjoy what I'm doing and look forward to working. I also know that if I scaled back my publishing and freelance work so that I was working only forty hours a week, I would immediately use those freed-up hours to spend more time writing books.

One day I hope to earn enough income through my books to pay the bills. I can stop freelancing and stop publishing periodicals. Then my sole work focus will be on books. The question that remains is, will I do this for forty hours a week or fifty-five? Stay tuned for the answer.

The Birds Are Singing

I've worked at home for years. With a home office, it's critical to have a professional, work-like environment. This is especially true when on a phone call (or video call). There can be no household noises, such as blaring TVs or radios, crying children, barking dogs, or talking spouses. Callers hear everything.

This was never an issue for me.

Then I moved my office from a windowless room in the basement to an unused bedroom on the main floor. When the weather is nice, I open the window for some fresh air.

But one time during a phone call, the person I was talking to asked, "Do I hear birds?"

Indeed, she did. Songbirds were serenading me. Though melodic and soothing, they were also quite loud. But I would have never guessed my caller would hear their unrestrained happiness.

Singing birds may be unprofessional, but I'm okay with that.

There Has to Be a Better Way

I don't know if I wasn't listening or am slow to catch on, but it wasn't until later in life that I realized how to land a job:

- The purpose of a resume is to secure an interview.
- The purpose of an interview is to sell yourself well enough to receive a job offer.
- The purpose of an offer is to negotiate a compensation package for your new job.

Silly me.

I thought that people should hire me because I could do the work—and would do it well. I wouldn't have applied if I didn't believe that.

I viewed the application/resume and interview steps as unnecessary irritations in the process. As far as the compensation negotiation, just skip that part and pay me what I'm worth.

The sad reality is that—except for a few positions, such as sales or marketing—being able to pen a compelling resume or conduct a convincing interview is no measure of a person's ability to do the work. It is solely their ability to obtain a job. The result is that employers hire unsuited people and overlook good candidates.

The same is true in politics.

A politician needs the ability to raise money, campaign, and debate well to raise poll numbers. And the candidate must speak with conviction to create interest among the electorate. But these skills have little bearing on their ability to govern well.

Whether it is obtaining a job or getting elected, the conventional processes do not allow the best person to prevail. There must be a better way.

Maybe there is. In the Bible, God picked his people's leaders. Hmm.

Partner or Employee?

Several years ago, after much planning and consideration, my bride joined me in my publishing business. Her long commute to her job had become wearisome, and with winter approaching, bad weather would make it even longer and more worrisome.

As we shared this possibility with others, people responded with raised eyebrows and skepticism. One doubtful friend directly stated, "Married people should not work together."

A wise friend, however, advised that we consider whether my wife would be my employee or my partner. That was a great question. After much discussion, we opted for being partners.

We even did a trial run when she had some vacation time she needed to use. The test went quite well, so we moved forward with our plans. We were both pleased with the results. It was a good move, and I wish we had done it sooner.

The only occasional hiccups were that sometimes she acted like an employee, and sometimes I treated her as one. Even so, we proved that spouses can successfully work and live together.

However, we never fully realized the partnership goal. I think she enjoyed the lesser pressure of being an employee. Still, she persisted in working with me, even for a couple of years when I couldn't pay her. When a new opportunity popped up, she successfully transitioned from working with me to working in the public sector. She's much more suited for that work. She also enjoys it more than being cooped up in our home office with me all day.

God created us to work, so we should find a place that fits best for how he made us.

Six Years Too Late

A few years before we started working together, my bride received a "five-year plaque" at work—and she was miffed.

The public recognition for five years of work is supposed to be a good thing. Causing angst wasn't the intention. The goal of the award was to make her feel appreciated, to give her a reason to feel good about her job and the organization she worked for.

Sadly, it had the opposite effect. You see, she received the five-year plaque after eleven years of employment. The recognition came six years too late. Even more tragic, none of her coworkers realized the mistake.

I encouraged her to get the error fixed. If, for any future reason, her employment tenure needed verification, her company should give accurate information.

This discrepancy between reality and their computer database gave me pause. It's often claimed that people lie on their resumes and job applications. While I'm sure there are plenty of grand embellishments and outright fabrications that arise when seeking a job, I wonder how many of these alleged lies are poor corporate recordkeeping.

If she were to put on a job application or credit application that she had been employed for eleven years, but the company would confirm only five, who would the inquirer believe? Would anyone even tell her of the discrepancy? I fear not. I suspect the organization would summarily reject her application, and she would never know why.

After a bit of digging, we found her first W-2 from eleven years ago. She showed it to human resources, and with a couple of key clicks, they fixed the error.

She was then due her ten-year plaque, and it would be only one year late.

Fortunately, God is never late.

Checkmate

I pulled my chessboard out to play a game. It had been gathering dust for years. I used to be good enough to beat most people most of the time. I figured it was like riding a bike, that I would pick up where I left off. Not so.

After making a series of errors in the first game, I realized I wasn't as patient a player as I once was. I lost the first game—and then two more. I don't recall ever losing three games in a row.

With increased resolve and a commitment to focus, I started the fourth game strong. But after establishing a superior position, my play became haphazard, and I dug myself into a hole. My friend offered an intriguing gambit, and I went for it. Though he played his endgame without fault, I somehow emerged victorious. Garnering one win out of four, however, wasn't the outcome I expected.

Though I hate to lose, I was happy for my opponent. But being happy for my opponent's win at my expense is a hard perspective to balance.

However, my difficulty in concentrating dismayed me. The culprit, I fear, is years of trying to multitask, which is really an illusion. Now, I can rarely concentrate on a single chore without spurious thoughts invading my focus.

My work and my chess game are among the victims.

That is why when I write—or do any other work of importance—I must be in a distraction-free zone. Even the smallest interruptions take me from what I am doing, breaking my focus and causing me to make poor decisions.

Can You Disconnect?

A growing number of people can't survive without their smartphones. They have a compulsion to stay connected 24/7. When they go on vacation, they won't leave without their technology. They suffer from anxiety when they're electronically disconnected from the rest of the world. The thought of unplugging causes panic and a foreboding sense of loss and confusion.

In a way, I understand this. Technology is an essential element of my work. Without it, I couldn't accomplish anything. For those rare times when I lose my internet connection, I find little work I can do without going online.

Yet, when I end my workday, I can make it without being on the internet. Yes, the World Wide Web is a nice tool and a convenient resource, but it's just a tool, nothing more. It's not essential to life and living. I can survive without it.

On one trip, I chose to not lug my laptop. (By design, I can't access email from my smartphone.) As such, I went ninety hours without checking email. What a pleasant break. True, I paid for it when I returned home, with hundreds of messages clamoring for my attention and requiring a full day to wade through, but the respite from the information superhighway was wonderfully refreshing.

Frankly, despite my great affection for technology and constant use of it at work, I look forward to those times when I can set it aside and live life without the internet, social media, and email. I do this for most of every Sunday. It's part of my Sabbath rest.

I can disconnect, can you?

I Can't Wait to Go to Work

What's the first thing you think of when you wake up in the morning? This isn't a trick question.

Each morning my mind races beyond my early morning routine of exercise, Bible study, and breakfast. I immediately think of what I will do after that. What amazing work will I get to do today? It's exhilarating. And even for those days when the tasks before me are less than ideal, I know I'll get the chance to do something truly exciting.

But before I get out of bed and move into the day, I give my plans and expectations over to Papa. I ask for his favor as I navigate my work. I plead for Holy Spirit inspiration for what I will write. And I ask that God will be a real and tangible presence as I move through the day.

Most days unfold exceedingly well, but not every day is perfect. Some hold challenges and others present disappointments. Yet I know that the next day offers a new hope when I will again ask God for his blessings on all that I do. Because of inviting God into my day, I view all the work I do as spiritual, from listening to the Holy Spirit's insight so I can form the next sentence, to sending out an invoice, to strategically planning for the next year.

God created me to work and gave me work I love. That's why I can't wait to go to work each day. But if I try going without him, it would all be for naught.

I Am a Writer

I've been writing most of my life and had my first piece published when I was in my early twenties. Yet for most of my life, I never considered myself a writer, and I certainly didn't consider myself a creative person. Writing has always been a part of my adult life, both for work and for fun.

After decades of writing, I began to wonder if I was a writer. Maybe I was. But I still couldn't say it. My mind couldn't even form those words, let alone make my lips move to voice them.

But a few years ago, I realized I had to push past this. In the quiet of my office, with no one around, I forced myself to mumble the words, "I am a writer." They came forth as a mere whisper, one I could barely hear, and they lacked even the smallest hint that I believed it.

I tried again, this time a bit louder. It took me several more attempts before I spoke the words at a normal volume. Even then I didn't believe what I said. I felt like a poser and the biggest liar of all times. Still I persevered.

It took me several months before I mustered the courage to tell someone, "I am a writer." It was a pathetic effort, of that I'm quite sure. Yet I persisted. Each time I said those four words, they came a bit easier and carried a bit more certainty.

Now I say them with confidence, void of any guilt that I'm deluding myself or lying to others by claiming to be a writer.

I've come to realize that writing is art. Just as there are visual arts and performance arts, there are also written arts. That makes me an artist and a creative person.

Though I never embraced the idea that I had a creative bone in my body, I now realize that I can create using words. My Creator made me to be creative. Who would have thought?

Why I Write

Though I wrote poetry as an angst-filled teenager, I set it aside as an adult. Yet when I delve back into it, I'm often rewarded with acknowledgment and publication.

The first poem I wrote as an adult was a haiku, which I submitted to a writing contest. My concise seventeen-syllable creation was a finalist and published in *Imagine This! An ArtPrize Anthology*. This was the first time I considered myself a creative person.

For purists, haikus aren't supposed to carry a title, but mine did:

Why I Write

Linking letters and
wielding words to create art
for God, my Patron.

10.

❖

Money

> *For the love of money is a root of all kinds of evil. Some people, eager for money, have wandered from the faith and pierced themselves with many griefs (1 Timothy 6:10).*

Many people think the Bible condemns money. It doesn't. The Bible warns about the *love* of money, about making it a priority, about worshiping it. The pursuit of money can cause people to turn their backs on God. An improper attitude toward money can pile heartache upon heartache.

In the following pages I share some thoughts on money to help get us back on track regarding its proper place in our lives. We need to start by realizing our relationship with money is a spiritual issue.

How Much Is Enough?

Someone reportedly asked John D. Rockefeller, "How much money is enough?"

"Just a little bit more," he answered.

This push for more has propelled people to achieve some amazing accomplishments, but left unchecked, it can leave a wake of devastation—destroying lives, organizations, and resources. Left unexamined, it can ravage our souls.

When the push for more focuses on wealth, many people are never satisfied. Seeking more can become an inescapable snare.

Many people live beyond their means. They desire just a little bit more. They are, in fact, greedy.

A few people live within their means. They spend responsibly, not letting their reach exceed their grasp. But even these people are often one paycheck away from the collapse of their subsistence. They are living on the edge. Financial disaster waits at their door.

It's rare for people to live beneath their means, to live more simply than their checkbook balance says they can afford. They save money and give money away for good, God-honoring causes. They are wise.

Whichever category we find ourselves in, we'll do well to ask, how much is enough?

Do we need to make any changes in the way we live or with our attitudes toward money?

Living Beneath Your Means

Let's build on this thought.

My wife and I were talking with a young engaged couple and the subject of finances came up. I shared my thoughts, and in doing so, I gave them something to ponder.

I said that most people in the United States (and other first-world countries) live beyond their means. They misuse credit, are financially overextended, and one little glitch sends their world crumbling.

A few people live within their means. That is, they spend their money wisely, save for a rainy day—which will eventually happen—don't try to keep up with everyone else (those living beyond their means), are careful using credit, and make sensible investments. In short, they live fiscally responsible lives.

My goal, however, is to live beneath my means. That is, to live more simply than I can afford to. This certainly doesn't imply I've taken a vow of poverty or anything of the sort. But I have sworn off extravagance and am content with what I have, be it home, car, clothes, or other possessions. It's freeing not to always strive for more stuff, not to yearn for what's unneeded. That doesn't mean I don't have financial goals—I do. But they aren't materialistic in nature. I've learned that possessions weigh me down and make demands on my time, attention, finances, or mental state (that is, worry). Besides, we really don't own anything anyway. Things often own us.

So let's keep it simple. A financially prudent life is a whole lot less stressful and more God-honoring.

Are You Wealthy?

Are you wealthy? Your initial answer may be the same as mine was: no! But I've since learned that I was wrong. I recently saw a new reality concerning my relative financial well-being in this global economy.

Go to globalrichlist.com to see how you rank. The site considers your annual income compared with the rest of the world. In this regard, I suspect you'll find you are indeed well-off. True, quite a few people earn more than you, but many, many more are paupers in comparison.

If you haven't checked it out yet, you might be interested to know that if you made $32,000 (USD) last year, you are in the top 1 percent of the world's wealthiest people. You are a one-percenter. Who would have thought?

If you made $11,000, you will still be in the top 15 percent worldwide.

If you made $1,300 a year, you would be in the top half.

This knowledge certainly changed my perspective.

Let's develop a new attitude. We must stop comparing ourselves to that small minority who are better off than we are. It will only make us crave more stuff.

Instead, we should compare ourselves to that huge majority who are in greater need than we are. This will surely encourage us to give more. In doing so, we can make a difference in their lives and ours.

We Must Change Our Attitude toward Money

During the last economic downturn, I encouraged my blog readers to change some things about our financial perspective:
- Learn to be happy with less. Virtually everyone in the United States (and other first-world countries) is better off than half of the world's population.
- Don't spend what we don't have. Satisfying today's urges with tomorrow's income is courting disaster, especially since we have no control over our future or the money we could earn.
- Plan financially. This includes having an emergency fund and a retirement plan.
- Whenever possible, avoid debt. When this isn't feasible, pay off debt as quickly as possible.
- Use charge cards only as a convenience when making purchases. Do not use credit to buy things when we have no money. The first month we can't pay the balance in full means we're living beyond our means. Cancel the card, and don't apply for any more.
- Shun greed.

Greed was the root cause of the last economic downturn. I hear a chorus of cheers. Wait. Don't blame corporate greed. Although corporations are legal entities, they can't think and act on their own. People control corporations, and many of those people are greedy.

But the real culprit is the stockholders who demand higher returns on their investments. They are greedy.

Most everyone with a 401(k), IRA, money market account, CD, and any interest-bearing investment—many of which are tied to the stock market, either directly or indirectly—wants to make as much as they can. What starts as a desire to be good stewards of the money God blesses us with can easily morph into a greedy desire to maximize our return on investment (ROI).

Instead, let's seek to be happier with what we have and not seek more.

Needs Versus Wants

For several years I taught budget classes to people struggling with their finances. To help people move from dependency to self-sufficiency, we looked at two areas: the amount of money coming in and the amount of money going out: income versus spending.

The quickest way to help people with financial struggles is to show them how to spend less. This requires distinguishing between wants and needs.

People have three basic physical needs: food, shelter, and clothing. We and our churches will do well to aid the people who lack these needs. Beyond that, everything else constitutes wants. Seriously.

I see no moral obligation to help people get the things they *want* but can't afford.

Between obvious needs and frivolous wants sits a continuum of financial considerations. For example, transportation is not a basic need, but people do need a way to get to and from work each day so they can earn money to pay for the things they need. There are many transportation options, and the first option we think of may not be the best solution. A bike might do or a good pair of walking shoes. What about public transportation or asking someone for a ride? It's not true that people *need* a car to get to work. They *want* a car to get to work, but they can often meet their need for transportation in other creative ways.

I worked with financially struggling people who couldn't pay their monthly bills, but refused to cancel their cable subscriptions, give up their smartphones, or stop eating out every day. They insisted on keeping cars they couldn't afford, living in houses with mortgages they couldn't pay, and sending their kids to private schools when there were other viable options. These are all wants, and these people expected someone to help them fulfill their wants.

Those in financial turmoil, as well as those who aren't, should evaluate their spending. We need to distinguish between wants and needs, adjusting our expectations appropriately. It's a spiritual issue.

End Poverty

From time to time, I hear about some group that wants to "end poverty" or "stamp out poverty." I don't give much thought to such goals because they will never happen—they can't. But before I explain why, let me share two similar-sounding initiatives that are *more* important and *can* happen:

Clean Drinking Water: About one billion people lack access to clean drinking water. This causes illness, disease, and preventable death. Many organizations work to address this, from drilling wells to offering water purification systems. The result is clean, safe drinking water for some of the world's most hurting people.

Clean drinking water is an issue we can solve and in which everyone can help, whether directly through action or indirectly by donating money to clean water initiatives.

Food for the Hungry: Reportedly 800 million to one billion people lack a basic supply of food. Sadly, experts on such things say that the world's farmers produce enough food to feed everyone. It's just not available where the people need it, or various governments, factions, or politics obstruct its distribution. Much of the problem boils down to transportation coordination and political corruption. This is a bit harder for us to personally tackle, but many organizations work to address world hunger. While most people can't directly help, anyone can donate money to feed a hungry person.

So clean drinking water and food for the hungry are serious problems that we can and should address.

Fighting poverty, while a noble cause, is of secondary importance to these more basic human needs. Besides, Jesus said there will always be poor people (Matthew 26:11).

The reason we will never end poverty is that it isn't an attainable goal. Ending poverty is about as feasible as a school wanting all their students to have above average grades. Although they can increase the overall academic level of performance, there will always be those who struggle, who will be below average academically.

In the same way, no matter how much the overall standard of living improves, some people will always be at the bottom—below average—who don't have as much as others. They will live under the label of impoverished.

Though we must help others with their *needs*, let's not delude ourselves into thinking we can ever make poverty go away.

Trust God

My bride and I set aside money for our future. We save for larger purchases and hold off buying them until we can pay in full. We also save for retirement, even though I don't plan on retiring and hope to write for the rest of my life.

With the preparation my bride and I have made for our future, it's easy to fall into the trap of trusting our bank account. This is foolish because we can never save enough money to cover every scenario. Instead, we need to put our future in God's hands and trust him with it.

Yes, God honors our planning. It would be irresponsible not to prepare for our future financial well-being, but it's also wrong to remove God from the equation.

We must trust God with our finances and our future. Anything else is folly.

Blessed to Be a Blessing

In the Bible, God tells Abraham that he, God, will bless him so that he, Abraham, can bless others (Genesis 12:2). Paul confirms this when he tells the people in Corinth that those who give generously will receive more and the stingy will receive less (2 Corinthians 9:6).

God provides for us financially. For some, this is a little, and for others, it's a lot. Regardless, we should use the money he blesses us with to first cover our needs and then to help others with their *needs*. Next, we can set money aside for our future. And last, we can look at the things we want.

May our wants be simple and our hearts generous to give to those in need.

11.

❖

Travel

> *He protected us on our entire journey and among all the nations through which we traveled (Joshua 24:17).*

I've never liked to travel. Though I like to visit other places, the effort to get there is something I force myself to endure. Some of my jobs required me to travel. And in the couple-year stint when I worked as a consultant, I traveled a lot. Though I accepted travel as a necessary part of the job and even developed a strategy to deal with it in a positive way, I never liked it.

Now I like to limit my trips to one day and accessible by car. I even announced to my family that my goal is never to fly again. Yep, I dislike it that much.

Even so, my travels have provided me with both opportunity and insight.

Three Stories about Flying

Like any traveler, I have many stories. Here are three.

A Private Flight: One time, while awaiting a connecting flight and anxious to return home, I sat at the sparsely-occupied gate, immersed in my crossword puzzle. Suddenly, an announcement interrupted my focus. "Now boarding all rows, all passengers for flight 3512. This is the final boarding."

Strange. I must have tuned out the previous announcements. Grateful that I heard this one, I walked alone to the gate and handed the agent my ticket. She smiled. "We wondered if you were here."

Perplexed at such a strange comment, I smiled back and proceeded through the doorway. The door shut behind me. Walking down the empty jetway, I stepped into the plane. The flight attendant informed me that I was the only passenger.

She asked if I would be needing beverage service. I thanked her and joked that she could take the night off. "Does this happen very often?"

"Occasionally," she replied. "Once the plane was empty. But we flew anyway so it would be ready for an early flight the next day."

For the price of a normal commercial ticket, I had a private flight with a personal flight attendant.

Priority Clearance: While anxiously waiting for my flight to my connecting hub—where I had a tight forty-minute layover—I heard a series of announcements no traveler wants to hear. The first announcement claimed the delay would be thirty minutes, then another announcement said it would be an hour, and then . . . well, you probably know the scenario. Finally, two hours past the scheduled departure, we had boarded and were ready to taxi. Then the copilot made an unusual announcement. "This is the captain's final flight for the airline. He's retiring after twenty-two years of service."

As was the tradition in these cases, we would taxi past two fire trucks, which would spray a canopy of water over and on the plane. As we proceeded parallel to the terminal, airline personnel lined the windows and waved their goodbyes. Soon, passengers began waving back.

Then came another surprise announcement. "Because this is the captain's final flight, ground control has given us priority clearance for departure. We're next in line for takeoff." Never have I experienced such a speedy departure. The runway even pointed us toward our destination. In a couple of hours, another announcement came through the speakers. "We have enjoyed a strong tail wind and are preparing for landing. Because this is the captain's final flight, air traffic control has given us priority clearance to land."

Again, it was a straight shot to the runway, and we quickly touched down. Then came a third unexpected announcement. "Because this is our captain's final flight, ground control has given us priority to taxi to our gate."

Could it be? I made my connection!

A Long Cab Ride: I was flying home with two coworkers. It was winter. We landed at our connecting hub only to learn that our final flight, the last of the day, was canceled due to weather. The more experienced travelers snapped up all the rental cars. We'd have to spend the night there and fly home the next day. This was the last thing I wanted to do. Also, one of my associates was sick and the other planned to start her vacation the next morning, with an early flight out for a cruise. If we delayed until the next day, she would miss her flight and part of the cruise.

No more flights, no buses, and no rental cars were available. We were 150 miles from home. We were desperate. Outside, a city employee orchestrated cab rides. "What would be the possibility of getting a cabbie to take us to Kalamazoo?" I asked.

Glancing at our tired faces, she smiled. "Let me find you a good ride." After putting local fares into the next five cabs, a nice, new cab with a competent-looking driver pulled up. "This is your cab." She smiled and made a grand wave toward our coach. She had a preliminary discussion with the bewildered cabbie. Once I assured him that I could provide directions, we were off. Four hours later he dropped us off at our home airport. I paid the $380 fare. Later the airline refunded our unused tickets, so the net cost of our 150-mile cab ride was only $30.

I have many stories I could have shared, but I picked these for a reason. Each one has a positive outcome. May we always seek to find the positive in everything we do, especially the things we don't like to do.

Travel Mode

To successfully travel, I need to be in travel mode. It's my strategy to survive. It has three parts:

Have a Plan: If I don't have a plan to occupy the idle time when I'm waiting to board or while I'm in the air, I'll become bored and irritable. My plan starts with having magazines to read. As I finish each one, I throw it away, making my load a little lighter. Reading magazines is great for standing in line and before takeoff. I listen to podcasts while waiting at the gate and on the flights. When in flight, I do crossword puzzles in airline magazines. Movies, another favorite pastime, are welcome on longer flights. Finally, I reward myself at each hub with a snack, either frozen yogurt or popcorn.

Be Realistic: I used to expect that an airline schedule represented what would happen. The fact that airlines begin padding their schedules to boast a higher on-time arrival did little to erase my frequent disappointment.

Then I realized that a more reasonable attitude was to assume the plane would be late and celebrate an on-time arrival. Here's why. Let's say a trip has two legs of the flight going and two returning. If one leg is late, do you remember the three that were on time? No, you dwell on the one that was late.

Look at it mathematically. Assume each flight has an on-time arrival of 70 percent. That means that for the two legs of the flight to get to your destination, you have only a 49 percent chance that both legs will be on time. Add to that the two legs of your return flights, you have only a 24 percent chance of all four planes being on time. And if your journey includes three legs in each direction, your odds of all six being on time drop to 11 percent.

Setting realistic expectations lessens my chances of disappointment. This isn't optimism versus pessimism. It's realism.

Make the Most of It: Though I never fully got there, I tried to adopt a perspective of adventure when I traveled. Then I'm more apt to remember the positive—as with my three flying stories. When traveling, I have a chance to meet people I'll never see again, yet my encounter with them makes a memorable impression. Hopefully, I can do the same for them.

A simple kindness offered or received uplifts spirits. Even spending time to check out the airport architecture has its rewards.

When traveling, as with life, to realize a positive outcome, have a plan, be realistic, and make the most of it.

Breakfast in Seattle

On Sunday morning I needed to leave for my convention by 7 a.m. To my dismay, the hotel's kitchen didn't open until 7. The front desk had no options for my morning meal, the most important meal of the day.

I recalled seeing a McDonald's a few blocks away. At 6:30 I set off on a brisk walk, praying that Mickey D's would be open. The streets in downtown Seattle were mostly quiet and the sidewalks empty. My hope that the Golden Arches would be serving breakfast faded.

I approached the restaurant, and much to my glee, the lights were on. Not only that, but a bustle of activity filled the place. They were doing a brisk business. What was unusual was that most of the patrons appeared to be homeless. (I know what to look for because I once volunteered at a homeless shelter.)

Although I was wearing a light jacket, most people had on winter coats (needed to keep warm at night). They wore mismatched clothes, tattered and dirty (the homeless accept whatever clothes people offer, can't color coordinate, and lack access to washing machines). Many carried worn plastic grocery bags bulging with contents, possibly their only possessions. A line at the bathrooms snaked through the restaurant (most homeless don't have access to restrooms at night). And there was a momentary outburst (perhaps alcohol-related but more likely the result of mental illness), but a friend quieted the ruckus.

The beautiful thing was that the McDonald's employees weren't a bit fazed. They treated everyone with respect and courtesy, not shooing people away or insisting that purchases be "to go." I'm sure non-paying people were present, too, just wanting to get warm, but no one objected.

This is how it should be but seldom is. Most restaurants don't want "undesirable" people in their establishments—even if they have money. Bathrooms are off limits, and they quickly ask such folks to leave.

For my part, I was happy for the experience, witnessing a business directly address a societal issue. In a satisfying way, this was church for me that day. I worshipped God by witnessing generosity, compassion, and community. In fact, I so enjoyed being there that I returned Monday morning to repeat the experience. Thank you, McDonald's, for doing the right thing.

Save Water

Most hotel rooms come with a "save water" card. They request that we conserve water (and avoid other environmentally-unfriendly actions) by permitting them to skip changing the bedsheets if our stay is more than overnight. Placing that card on the bed signifies your acceptance of their request.

In a similar manner, a notice in the bathroom suggests we indicate our willingness to reuse towels by hanging them on the shower rod.

I'm fine with both requests. We don't change the sheets daily at home. Same with towels. If weekly is acceptable at our house, it's okay at hotels—at least from a cleanliness standpoint. Saving water is good stewardship that honors God.

Of course, this disregards the high price paid for the privilege of staying there. It is arguable that at a couple hundred dollars a night, fresh linens are in order each day. And since my concessions save them time and money, I deserve a break on the price.

In considering this, I must point out that using water to wash a towel does not actually *consume* water—the way going for a drive consumes gasoline. Once the laundry process is complete, the water still exists, albeit in a slightly less clean condition. After treatment, we can use the water again—and again.

The claim of protecting the environment is a ruse. Their actual desire is to save time and money, thereby increasing profitability. I'm all for profits, but I don't hide that reality by falsely pretending to care about water.

How do I know they're disingenuous? Quite simply, most hotel rooms waste water: the faucets drip, the drain plugs don't work, the toilets run continuously, or the showers have problems, either diverting only a fraction of the water to the showerhead or coming out with such force as to peel your skin off, with no way to tame the flow.

At least one of these problems crops up in most every hotel room. Addressing them will save water too. But they don't make these repairs because that would take time and cost money.

Waiting for Sand

I understand the phrase "pounding sand" as a reference to futile activity, but "waiting for sand" is a new one to me.

While awaiting the takeoff of a small commuter plane, we endured a lengthy and unexpected delay. Finally, the pilot explained.

The plane was unbalanced, and the plane's tail section was too light. To correct this, they would add weight in the back. We were waiting for bags of sand to arrive so they could accomplish this.

If this weight imbalance was a safety issue, I welcome the delay. However, if they merely did it to make the plane fly more aerodynamically to save fuel, I'm a bit miffed.

Because of this delay, I missed my connecting flight, as I'm sure was the case for many of my fellow travelers who had even tighter connections.

As a result, I understand *waiting for sand* to mean a needless, unwarranted delay.

How often do we find ourselves *waiting for sand?* How often do we cause it?

Making Travel Connections

I view air travel as something to endure. As such, while my body is flying, my mind goes to my happy place—whatever that means. Therefore, I can miss opportunities around me. But sometimes I come out of my self-imposed cocoon and actually connect with my fellow travelers.

On one flight, I plopped down in my seat and the lady next to me blurted, "I'm kinda nervous. This is my first time flying." I assured her it would be fine and told her about the scheduled one-hour flight (thirty minutes on the ground and thirty minutes in the air). Once we landed, I showed her the monitors for connection information, walked her to her gate, and pointed out the closest restroom and nearest eatery (she had over two hours to fill). She thanked me profusely, and we parted company.

Over the years, I've helped many people navigate an airport. Interestingly, everyone was female. I guess that reinforces the stereotype that guys don't ask for help. (For the record, I'm not opposed to doing so, but only when I'm confident that my advisor won't make things worse.)

Later, on the hotel shuttle, I struck up a conversation with a guy. We talked about his business and then his family, which segued into some of his personal struggles. Conversation flowed easily. He would make a statement. I would respond with a thoughtful question. He would answer, and the process would repeat. I wasn't probing, but I was being intentional. I couldn't believe the details he shared, but if he wanted to talk, I would listen. I made some positive observations he hadn't realized and affirmed good in areas where he saw only frustration.

Suddenly, he said, "I can't believe I'm telling you all this. I just met you!" He paused and then raised an eyebrow. "You're not like an undercover guy, trying to find out stuff about me, are you?"

That's one I'd never heard. I assured him I wasn't. "Some people say I'm a good listener."

He beamed. "And I'm a good talker."

Most people are good talkers—if only someone will listen.

Who's in Control?

When my bride and I were returning from a trip, we allowed plenty of time to take the shuttle from the hotel to the airport—more than three hours for a fifteen-mile trek. However, a series of unforeseen events conspired against us, making our schedule tighter and tighter with each progressive twist.

As each delay transpired, it became less likely we would make it to our gate in time. I kept telling myself, "We will either make our flight or we won't, but there's nothing you can do about it. Therefore, you might as well just relax and watch events unfold."

My self-talk, however, was easier to think than to do. As the clock ticked down, I became more unnerved. Fortunately, the airport security was smooth and efficient—despite my forgetting to discard the bottle of water from my carry-on. (I intended to drink it with the breakfast we had to skip.)

We arrived at the gate, breathless, haggard, and hungry, mere seconds before the call for final boarding.

As we settled into our seats, I tried to calm my frayed nerves. I reminded myself that while we can't control the things that happen to us, we can control our reaction to them.

In fact, it's the only thing we can control—and I did a poor job of it.

12.

Personal

For you created my inmost being; you knit me together in my mother's womb (Psalm 139:13).

In the book of Genesis, the Bible tells us that God created us, both male and female, in his image. Later, David gives us a greater glimpse into what this entails. Our creation is not the general formation of our species. Instead, it's the specific design of each of us as individuals. David affirms that God created the innermost, intimate essence of who he is. David uses the imagery of God knitting him together inside his mother's uterus. For this, we get a sense that, although created in God's image, we are truly unique.

Following are some random reflections that reveal my God-given individuality. As you read them, may you celebrate your own uniqueness.

Age Is Not a Number but an Attitude

Many of my friends are younger than me, often by quite a bit. In fact, I'd rather spend time with people half my age than with my own demographic. I don't know what they think about hanging out with me, but it's great to be around them. I feel more alive when I'm with them because they act more alive.

Too many people my age have settled. They've accepted the status quo and are coasting toward nothingness, yet they don't even know it. How sad.

Many younger people, however, have a zest for living. Life is an adventure, and they're just beginning. They're learning, dreaming, growing. They're awash with wonder. I'm like that, and more so when I'm around them. Yes, experience may have tempered my zest a bit, but I'm still learning, dreaming, growing. That's life. The alternative is death. And I'm too young to think about that.

I once served on a committee with people my age and older. (For the record, they hadn't settled.) We discussed who to invite to join our group. Our leader made an astute observation: "There are no Millennials on our committee."

He offended me. *Wait, I'm a Millennial!* Then I corrected my silent words before embarrassing myself aloud. *No, you're not. You just think you are.*

Ah, the joy of delusion.

Yes, I identify more with Gen X and especially Millennials than I do the Baby Boomers that I am. (Gen Zers are cool too.) I skew a bit more toward the postmodern worldview of youth than I embrace the modern perspective people my age normally hold to.

Maybe I was born too soon. Or maybe I just have a young heart.

Either way, it doesn't matter, because age isn't a number. It's an attitude.

Cross Words

I have had a lifelong fondness for words. My avid reading of fiction as a child and teenager gave way to becoming a student of nonfiction as an adult. More recently I reclaimed my love of fiction. Along with that goes forty years of writing experience and twenty years as a magazine publisher. Given my affection for words, it should come as little surprise that I enjoy crossword puzzles.

When I work a puzzle, I rely solely on the mind: mine and sometimes my family's. (I used to tap all available non-human resources, but upon enduring merciless harassment after buying a crossword dictionary, I swore off artificial assistance.)

Unfortunately, I am, quite ironically, a poor speller. And my "flexible" pronunciation of many words doesn't help my spelling either.

My wife often endures the brunt of my spelling deficiencies. It might go something like this:

"How do you spell cat?"

"C-A-T"

"It's not with a "K?"

"No."

"Could it be four letters? Like K-A-T-T or K-A-I-T?"

"Ah, no!"

I ponder a bit more. "I can make kitty fit if it only has one T."

"No, there are definitely two Ts in kitty."

I contemplate the situation further, but I'm no longer thinking of a four-letter word for feline. Instead, I marvel that a person with orthography issues could so immensely enjoy crossword puzzles—and come so close to completing most of them.

Flipping Houses

Few people know that I once flipped a house. This was decades ago when I was in my early twenties. House flipping wasn't a thing then. In fact, the book I bought to guide my process called it house recycling. But the concept was the same: Buy an undervalued house in need of attention. Fix it up, and sell it for a profit.

I envisioned doing this the rest of my life. I might even do it full-time. Boy, was I delusional.

After careful research, I bought my first house for less than what many new cars sell for today. I planned my renovations, made a budget, and theorized what I could sell the refurbished product for.

Alas, it didn't work out that way. My budget was low, and my anticipated selling price too high. After one year of work, I sold it and about broke even. And this didn't account for all my labor.

Ironically, a few days after I had purchased the house, another interested buyer contacted me and offered to buy it for several thousand dollars more than what I had paid for it. It was tempting. I could have tripled my investment in less than a week. Instead, I wanted to pursue my dream of recycling a house. I turned him down.

A year later, I sold the house for the same price the guy had offered a year earlier. But in those intervening twelve months, I had spent thousands of dollars and countless hours working on my house—with no return on my investment.

Knowing what I know now, from my experience and after watching hundreds of house-flipping shows, I'm sure I could do better. However, I don't want to try. Flipping houses is a risky endeavor that requires lots of energy.

Some might say the same thing about writing books, but this is what I enjoy and, I believe, am good at. No one will ever be able to buy the houses I flip, but they will be able to flip through the books I write.

Thank you for doing that. You are why I write.

Break Needless Habits

Several years ago, I realized a ritual had crept into my morning hair-combing routine. This new activity added nothing to my final appearance, yet morning after morning, I persisted in this needless habit.

It took only a few seconds, and eliminating it did not increase my free time each day. I calculated the time I freed up through eliminating this habit gained me an extra thirty minutes per *year*.

Then I noticed another time-wasting habit while brushing my teeth. I streamlined my process with no change in the teeth-cleaning experience. This, however, was a harder habit to break.

Since then I've uncovered many unneeded rituals that have worked their way into my routine activities. Each time I spot one of these time wasters, I set about removing it and forming a streamlined process to replace it.

A couple of these uninformed habits relate to writing. One is to run spell check way too many times on the same piece. Though this provides satisfaction each time I do it, it's a waste of time. I now strive to spell-check a piece only twice: once early in the process and once at the end.

Another habit is adding two spaces at the end of every sentence, which I learned in high school typing class. This is no longer standard procedure, however, so I decided to retrain myself and use only one space to end each sentence. To my utter shock and total glee, it took only a couple days to retrain myself.

Though the amount of time saved by not double spacing at the end of every sentence is negligible, even after several hundred thousand sentences, I do know that there's a cumulative benefit from *all* the needless activities I've eliminated from my life. As a result, I have less to do and am more productive.

The Third Time's the Charm

I vote at every election. Not only is it my duty to do so, but I believe that if I don't vote, I have no right to complain about what happens.

At a local school election, three people ran for school board. Also on the ballot was a millage renewal. It was about as simple as a ballot could be. I did my homework and was ready to vote. At the polling precinct, I filled out the paperwork, showed my ID, and received my paper ballot.

In a hurry, I didn't look at the names on the ballot. I intended to vote for the first and third candidates. At least they were the first and third alphabetically. Alas, the ballot wasn't in alphabetical order. I marked the first name on the ballot only to discover he wasn't one of my chosen candidates.

I told the election official about my mistake. Could I have a new ballot? He was most accommodating, but doing so took longer than the original process of getting my first ballot. They had to put my "soiled" ballot in a special folder to document my error. To my embarrassment, after nearly twelve hours of polling, the folder was empty. I was the first voting-challenged person of the day.

I cast my votes on the new ballot and turned it in, only to learn that there was one open seat, not two. I had spoiled my second ballot.

I repeated the process of getting a second replacement ballot. I voted the third time, this time correctly.

My bride completed her voting and picked up an "I Voted" sticker. She offered one to me. I declined, at which point the election official quipped, "He can have three."

This amused everyone. I just wanted to get out of there as fast as possible.

How Much Does It Cost?

I'm not one who spends money easily or frivolously. It should surprise no one that at some point in a purchase decision I will deliberate on the cost of the item:
- Can I afford it?
- Is this a wise use of my money?
- Will I derive enough value from it?
- Is this an emotional or intellectual decision?
- If I buy this item now, will it keep me from making a more relevant purchase later?

Yeah, I do that.

When I'm at a restaurant, I also look at prices.

For the first part of my life, price was a practical concern. Did I have enough money to pay the bill? I could order only what I could pay for with cash, be it with bills or change—often it was change.

Though I never want to overpay for a meal, the primary reason I look at prices now is that I perceive price as an indicator of quantity. You see, Mom insisted I eat everything on my plate and not waste a bite. ("There are starving children in India," I heard more than once.) Therefore, I'm compelled to eat what the restaurant gives me, even if I'm full.

If the portion is too big, I eat too much. So I judge the amount of food by the cost of the meal. Though not an error-free method, it always saves me money and often helps keep my waistline in check.

Black and White in a Technicolor World

I dream in black and white. I assumed this is because I grew up watching black-and-white TV. Lately, I've noticed that occasionally my black-and-white dreams contain one item in color—a more recent cinematic effect that my dreaming emulates. A couple of times an entire dream scene blasts with vibrant, blinding color. It comes as such a surprise that I wake up.

Since I grew up watching television in black and white and dream in black and white, it shouldn't surprise anyone that I enjoy black-and-white movies. (And for the record, I'm not a purist, so I don't object to the colorization of black-and-white films. A good movie is a good movie, regardless.)

Several years ago, I was again watching the black and white classic *To Catch a Thief*. One scene has Grace Kelly wearing a stunning white gown and adorned by a sparkling array of diamonds encircling her stately neck. Just then, my son—who was in middle school at the time—walked into the room. "What are you watching?"

I provided more information about this classic tale than he wanted to hear or needed to know. I then gushed about Grace Kelly and concluded by saying, "Isn't she incredible?"

He stood silently for several moments, shook his head, and said, "I just don't get it."

How could he? I'm sure he dreams in color.

How Many Friends Do You Have?

How many friends do you have?

For many, a quick answer resides in social media. In addition to Facebook "friends," some might consider Twitter followers, LinkedIn connections, and Instagram followers as friends. But the number of online friends overstates the situation.

Try removing social media from consideration. For a revised answer, people may count the number of email addresses in their email accounts or the number of contacts in their smartphones. But this still overstates things.

Let's remove all technology from consideration. How many friends do you see face-to-face on a regular basis? But is everyone in this group truly a friend?

For me, my true friends are those I could call in an emergency. It's a short list.

What does your friend list look like?

A Picture Is Worth a Thousand Words

When I write, I am compulsive about frequently saving my work. One time my computer locked up when I was writing a column. I hadn't saved my work for about five minutes.

Occasionally words come slow and birth with difficulty. Other times, they flow fast and with good results. Sometimes, I get in the zone. Not only do the words come quickly, but they are good words in a clever order that project profound ideas in a compelling manner.

When my computer locked up, I had been in the zone. I was devastated. The thought of losing my eloquent prose was unacceptable.

Hoping for the unlikely, I took a break, with the improbable wish that my computer would work when I returned, allowing me to save my file. It didn't.

Out of desperation, however, comes innovation. I took a picture of my computer screen.

Then I rebooted and rekeyed my brilliant words.

They say a picture is worth a thousand words. In my case, it was only a couple hundred, but they were good words I couldn't bear to lose. Thanks to a camera, I didn't have to.

Thank you, Holy Spirit, for an elegant solution to a frustrating problem.

How Secure Are Those Security Questions?

I appreciate the efforts financial institutions go through to keep my account—and the information behind it—safe. These steps include multi-page sign-in procedures, using two-factor authentication, or requiring a security code. Yes, it's a hassle, but it's a hassle I'll happily endure to protect my information. What perplexes me, however, are the security questions. They are either too simple or too hard.

Some security questions are in the category of too easy, such as what high school I went to. Anyone can find basic facts about me online. The same is true for my favorite food. Those who know me would answer pizza. Other questions are about my mother's maiden name, where I lived in third grade, and so on.

The impossibly hard questions are those that have multiple answers. For example, what street did you grow up on? What was your favorite pet's name? Or what color was your first car? For each of these, I have two equally valid answers. I moved while growing up; among scores of pets, two dogs tie as my favorite; and as far as my first car—I had it painted. Should I cite the starting color or the ending color?

Other hard questions are those that change over time. Examples include my favorite color, my best teacher, my preferred ice cream flavor, my all-time favorite movie, or my favorite TV show. Then to compound the whole issue, I need to spell the answers correctly (challenging for my dogs' names) and remembering if I capitalized any of the letters ("School" or "school") or used abbreviations (such as "W" or "West;" "Ave" or "Avenue").

However, I have a good solution for this. I simply made up an answer, random and completely secret. I use this for every security question. For example, I might pick "MyrtleBeach45" as my answer.

Q: What's your favorite food? A: MyrtleBeach45

Q: What color was your first car? A: MyrtleBeach45

Q: On what street did you grow up? A: MyrtleBeach45

Q: Is your security question really secure? A: MyrtleBeach45

By the way, MyrtleBeach45 is not the right answer to my security question.

However, some places won't let you give the same answer to multiple security questions. I'm still working on a solution to that problem.

I don't know if all this makes my online information more secure or not, but I feel better about it.

13.

Pursuing Competence

Not that we are competent in ourselves to claim anything for ourselves, but our competence comes from God (2 Corinthians 3:5).

In this collection of reflections, the theme is varying sorts of competence. Paul reminds us that our competence comes from God, with the implication that there's a spiritual component in all that we do. May we have eyes to see it.

Words Can Tear Down or Build Up

A friend entering a master's program took a pass-fail class designed to weed out weaker and mismatched students from the program. After spending less than ten minutes in one-on-one communication, the professor deemed him ill-suited for the program and its associated profession. The professor summarily failed my friend. Although discouraged, my friend repeated the class with another instructor, who declared him functioning at the PhD level.

Another friend wrapped up her last semester of college with student teaching. Things proceeded well, and her mid-semester report glowed with affirmation. Imagine her dismay when her mentor's final assessment determined she wasn't fit to teach. My friend never rebounded from this hit to her self-esteem. She never taught again but, instead, selected a different career.

Although both examples come from the field of education, the lesson isn't unique to that area. Anytime someone has power over another, their words carry a great deal of weight—so much so that people may abandon their career choices or have their confidence destroyed.

If you must deliver discouraging news, make sure the recipient knows why. Explain your reasons. Salt it with something positive. And most important, never abandon them when they are at their weakest.

It is far better to use our positions of power to encourage others, build them up, and strengthen them. Imagine my friend and how hard he will work now that he is secure in the knowledge that he's functioning at the PhD level.

Imagine my other friend who abandoned her dream to teach. How many students will never learn what she could have taught them? Will she spend the rest of her life wondering "what if"?

With power comes responsibility. Use it well.

A College Education for Everyone

A few years ago, there was a concerted political push in the United States to increase homeownership rates. The idea was to help renters become buyers. This would have many benefits for those who made the jump, including an increased standard of living, greater self-esteem, and financial security (by building up equity).

However, many people who shouldn't have bought houses were pushed into doing so. Sub-prime loans exacerbated the situation, with the assumption that balloon payments wouldn't be a problem and the belief that the housing bubble wouldn't pop. These forces conspired together to create a perfect storm for economic disaster.

The truth is, not everyone should own a home.

Now the political emphasis has switched from owning a home to getting a college degree. Indeed, the current refrain is "a college education for everyone." Never mind that not everyone is college material. Some need to pursue a trade, join the service, or directly enter the workforce. Sending the ill-equipped, unmotivated, or uncaring to college will do nothing to improve their lives. However, it will saddle them with student loans, as well as take the place of someone who should be there.

In addition, if everyone got a college degree, then those seeking to distinguish themselves will be pushed into grad school. Indeed, some fields are already like that.

If this effort to send everyone to college succeeds, the result will not be the graduates getting better jobs, but merely an upward push on required qualifications, as well as more money spent on schooling and increased student debt. Some people claim that the financial value of a degree has already declined, without providing an acceptable return on investment.

It will be only a matter of time before the college bubble bursts—just like the housing bubble before it.

If you know someone contemplating college, you can help guide them to make the right decision for the right reasons, one that best fits their needs and goals. And if you are considering college, don't feel pressured to do what everyone else is doing. Instead, pursue the path that feels right for you.

Road Rage

Early in our marriage, my bride and I headed home from work, making a detour for groceries. I drove down the area's busiest street, full of rush-hour traffic, and attempted to pull into the left turn lane. Due to various reasons, I made a couple of partial forays into it, only to return to the lane for regular traffic. This infuriated the driver behind me, who sounded his disapproval through the liberal use of his truck's horn.

Once we were fully into the left turn lane, he roared past us when my spitfire wife stuck out her tongue. This sent him into a full-on fury. He screeched to a halt in the middle of rush hour and opened his truck door hard into the side of our car. He ran around to my driver's side door and challenged me to a fight in the middle of the road.

Being of sound mind—and a bit of a pacifist—I stayed in the car. This irritated him further. He lurched toward the driver's door and cocked his arm. Just then, oncoming traffic cleared. I gunned the engine as he swung his fist at my window. Instead of breaking my window and hitting me, he ended up shattering the rear window, spraying glass throughout the car. As I sped away, he returned to his truck to give chase.

We drove around the store's parking lot, playing cat-and-mouse between the rows of cars. Eventually, I maneuvered to the front of the grocery store, letting my bride escape and summon help. She was sure she was going to become a widow. As for me, I figured I could continue playing "keep away" until the police arrived—or I ran out of gas.

Fortunately, I was too cagey for him, and he soon gave up the chase. One witness got his license plate number and a bored cabby followed for a while to make sure he wasn't coming back.

The police ran the plates.

The truck's owner had a history with them. They knew him well. They arrived at his home to find his right hand wrapped in a bloodied bandage. He confessed and admitted he was aiming for my head when he swung his fist. Later, he was found guilty. He had to pay court costs and make restitution.

God protected me that day. He helped me think clearly during a heart-pounding crisis. He gave me a plan to keep my wife safe and then to keep me from harm.

A Reliable Witness

After our car was a victim of road rage, a police officer took our statements. He asked if the assailant had walked around the front of our car or the back. My bride answered, "The front," and I replied, "The back." We exchanged incredulous glances, each concerned with the other's sanity.

I attributed our contradicting testimonies to the trauma of the situation. I later wondered if eyewitness testimony in a court of law could really be depended upon with any degree of accuracy.

I recalled this during our *52 Churches* journey when we visited a different Christian church every Sunday for a year. Each week as we drove home from church and later processed our experiences, we all too often recalled details differently. Usually, these were over trivial facts, but occasionally our conflicting observations were more significant.

Given this experience—in which we're focusing on making detailed and accurate observations, even to the point of taking notes—our recollections are suspect. The testimony given in any hearing or trial may be in error, even when we think we're telling the truth. And this is a real problem when the truth is essential, and lives are at stake.

My Mailbox Dilemma

One fall I received a strange notice from my US mail carrier, who determined that the location of my mailbox was unacceptable. What's perplexing is it had been like that for twenty years, so I'm not sure why it suddenly fell out of compliance.

He noted two problems with my once-acceptable mailbox: it needed to be eight inches higher and moved closer to the road by about the same amount.

What's interesting is that the official printed instructions included with his note said that "Whenever possible, boxes must be located so that carrier's vehicle is *off pavement* when serving them," but my carrier's handwritten note said, "Move your box *closer to the road* so I don't have to *leave* pavement."

Isn't that just like the government, providing conflicting instructions and expecting compliance?

This is quite a dilemma. Do I move it closer as my carrier requested or farther away as the formal instructions dictate?

My carrier's note further implied that if I didn't move it, I might not receive my mail *every* day in the winter. So on a warm, sunny fall afternoon, I worked up a sweat moving my mailbox to where my carrier wanted it. At the time, I quipped that if the snowplow takes out my mailbox, then I won't receive my mail on *any* days.

A few months later, that's exactly what happened. My mailbox was ruthlessly torn from its post and tossed into the snowbank by a passing snowplow.

Thankfully, the post remained, as the frozen ground would have made it impossible to set a new one. However, the temperature was 7°F (-14°C) and the wind chill hovered at -5°F (-20°C). Did I mention there are a couple feet of snow where my mailbox once was?

I'm so glad I moved it.

Haste Makes Waste

I pride myself in having the discernment of knowing when not to take shortcuts—those times when doing something the easy way could end up making more work. I also know which shortcuts are worthwhile.

However, one time while mowing the lawn, I did an uncharacteristically poor move. It was one born out of laziness, haste, or a combination thereof. It was a decision with a high likelihood of disaster.

I was hand mowing around my house with the push mower. I had neglected to first pick up the hoses. Upon seeing the first hose and not wanting to stop the mower, I tipped the deck up, carefully pushing it over the hose. Everything went as I hoped. At the back of the house, I repeated this process for a second hose. This time the results weren't pleasant, with bits of rubber flying in all directions. Now I had to stop.

For not wanting to take a few seconds to stop the mower and move the hose, I ended up spending half an hour going to the hardware store, buying a replacement fitting, and wrestling it into place. Now my hose is a few feet shorter.

Haste does indeed make waste. I hope I learned my lesson.

Fire

Once when standing in line at my bank, I noticed a commotion had occurred at the car wash next door. Several trucks were parked haphazardly around the building, with a couple of fire trucks beside it. The folks at the bank confirmed there had been a fire. Someone had carelessly flung a cigarette, which had started it.

It seems a bit ironic that a business that uses mass quantities of water would fall victim to fire.

The good news is that the fire department is across the street. The bad news is that it's a volunteer fire department. This means that although the equipment was nearby, the people to operate it weren't. As I understand, when the alarm sounds, the volunteers converge at the station until enough have arrived to operate a truck. Then they take off. The rest of the volunteers head for the fire. Hence the random positioning of trucks.

The fire damage was obvious, with blackened doors and an open roof. But most of the building stood intact. Even so, the fire department had encircled the building with yellow caution tape, thereby shutting down the business.

It took a while before it reopened.

This reminded me that when we bought and insured our house, my agent explained that our rate was in the highest category because we had a volunteer fire department. Statistically, this means slower response times, thereby allowing for greater damage. I sarcastically remarked that if my house caught on fire, the insurance company must assume it would be a complete loss. My agent nodded.

Fortunately, this wasn't the case for the car wash. Thank you, volunteer firefighters.

The Mathematics of Influence

I recently made a new friend. She is pursuing her PhD in mathematics. She has finished her course work and is working on her dissertation. Interestingly, at one point, I, too, wanted a PhD in mathematics, but she is the first person I've met to do it.

Aside from the math part, another intriguing aspect is what she's researching. At the risk of oversimplification, she is studying the teaching techniques used by those who teach the math teachers.

Consider that, depending on the circumstances, during their careers, the average teacher will directly influence 500 to 5,000 students.

And, again depending on the circumstances, during a career, the average teacher of teachers will directly influence 500 to 5,000 teachers—and thereby indirectly influence 250,000 to 25,000,000 students.

Now, if she can help these teachers of teachers be more effective, say 500 to 5,000 of them during her career, the span of her influence will be vast, beyond what is reasonable to calculate. That is a profound amount of influence one person can make. It is a real possibility that she could change the way the next generation learns math.

And if you're one who struggled with math in school, this should be welcome news.

14.

Serious Stuff

Look, I am coming soon! My reward is with me, and I will give to each person according to what they have done (Revelation 22:12).

We have a responsibility to our world, to the people around us. We have many ways we can accomplish this, some with greater impact than others. However, the idea that God will reward us according to what we have done in the life he gave us is sobering. It drives me to select the best things I can do to make this world a better place—for the people who live here and for the God who created us.

Absolutes or Absolution?

Going back some forty or fifty years, there began the assertion that there are no moral absolutes—a tenet of Postmodernism, which I don't accept. It claimed each person must decide for themselves what is right and what is wrong. Therefore, each person has the freedom to decide what is ethical—for them. With this perspective, it becomes amazingly simple to justify cheating, lying, stealing, and hurting others. Under the claim that there are no moral absolutes, we can do anything that brings us pleasure or power.

What a mess we've made by abandoning traditional moral behavior.

Even so, we are rightfully shocked when one person hurts another for the sport of it. Or when upper-middle-class teenagers commit armed robbery for the adrenaline rush it gives them. Or a harassed student who carries a gun to school to take revenge.

Each of these instances is real, and we see them repeated too many times. This, unfortunately, results from embracing the idea that there are no moral absolutes. Having no moral absolutes inevitably leads to what most people consider immoral behavior.

Our society reinforces this. More significantly, our schools promote it: that each person should choose what is right or wrong for themselves. Rampant immoral behavior results.

I suspect the thinking that first promoted this philosophy was a desire for sexual freedom, which required justification for promiscuous behavior to assuage guilt. However, to assert that there are no sexual moral absolutes, but that all other moral issues are absolute, is illogical. Therefore, to justify indiscriminate sexual behavior, the argument needed to extend itself to all moral issues, opening the door for acceptable cheating, lying, stealing, and killing.

What we have now is a quagmire of moral confusion and behavioral anarchy that has permeated our culture and threatened our future. It's not popular these days to claim that moral absolutes exist, but the alternative is the slippery slide we're on to immoral mayhem.

Let's take a stand for moral absolutes and the God who gave them to us.

A Sad Situation

Several years ago, a sixteen-year-old girl tragically died in a house fire—because her parents had chained her to her bed.

After they received appropriately long prison sentences for her death, the father vented to any who would listen. While he admitted to "a possible error in judgment" over chaining her to her bed, he justified his action as warranted.

According to reports, he said that his daughter's death wasn't his or his wife's fault. He launched into a tirade of blame. He accused the local school system, the children's protective service, the local law enforcement agency, and the state, asserting that they either knew about—or should have known about—the situation and should have intervened. These various authorities should have stepped in, he claimed, to help them properly raise their daughter and, therefore, prevent her unfortunate death.

I'm not sure what bothers me more, a chained child dying in a fire or the people who caused her death claiming it wasn't their fault.

It's too late to save the girl, and there's nothing we can do to help her parents, but we can still make a difference. It starts when we commit to assuming responsibility for our actions and refusing to blame others. Then we can encourage others to do the same.

With Freedom of Speech Comes Responsibility

One of the core tenets in the United States is a right we revere: freedom of speech.

Within very broad limits (such as not screaming, "Fire!" in a crowded room), we citizens enjoy the freedom to say what we want, when we want, and in the way we want. At least in theory.

But if everyone is talking, then no one is listening. The flip side of freedom of speech should be the responsibility to be quiet.

That doesn't mean we need to listen and consider every voice, but it does mean we need to show respect. Our freedom of speech doesn't permit us to yell louder than someone else, shouting them down and thereby denying them their right to speak.

Sadly, this happens too often today, especially when a voice advocates an unpopular belief or a politically "incorrect" view. This includes standing up for traditional values.

Society is losing sight of what freedom of speech entails. And if this happens completely, we might lose even more, including the very right itself.

Every voice has the right to speak their beliefs and opinions, even the unpopular ones. If we start limiting what the people on the fringes say, we could find someone else trying to limit what *we* say.

Homeless Statistics

When you consider the homeless, what do you think they're like? (You do think of the homeless, right?)

Though the numbers change from one area to another and shift over time, here is a statistical snapshot of the homeless near where I live:

- 32 percent of homeless adults are employed
- 37 percent of the homeless are children
- 27 percent of the homeless are single parents
- 30 percent have education beyond high school
- 24 percent experience chronic homelessness, suggesting that 76 percent are short-term homeless
- 11 percent of homeless adults were homeless as children

The first four stats are surprising, not fitting most people's stereotypical views of homeless demographics. In general, I don't think of the homeless as having jobs, children, and post-secondary school education.

The last two figures are appalling, showing that for some, homelessness is pervasive and even generational. Of course, the flipside is that for most, homelessness is a temporary condition, with the hope of overcoming it. The more help that is available, the quicker these people can get back on their feet and again provide for themselves.

Those of us with homes can express gratitude for our own shelters by helping those without homes to turn their lives around. We can do this by supporting and volunteering at churches, parachurch organizations, and nonprofits that help feed, house, transport, train, and support the homeless as they work toward reversing their situation.

No one can fix this problem alone, but by working together we can make a difference.

Avoid Poverty

Many have cited the following three steps to avoid poverty. The source is unclear but may have originated with Ron Haskins of the Brookings Institution.

Young people can avoid poverty if they follow three essential rules for success:

1. Complete at least a high school education
2. Work full-time
3. Wait until age twenty-one to marry, and get married before having a baby

People who follow all three rules have a 98 percent chance of not living in poverty. Furthermore, they have a 72 percent chance of joining the middle class.

Many people criticize this claim, some citing all manner of hate-filled motivations or ignorance. Yet if we look at this list, we know in our hearts that it's correct. It's common sense. We can also logically see how someone who ignores these three essentials places themselves on a path that will likely lead them to needing government assistance and living a life of poverty.

What can we do to encourage teenagers to embrace these three essential rules? Beyond that, what can we do to help those who didn't or couldn't follow them and find themselves in need? I'm thinking especially of the teenage mom left to care for her children on her own.

These are big questions without clear answers, but a good place to start is to find an organization already addressing one of these areas and working with them to make a difference.

An Epic Fail

The purpose of unions is to create and protect jobs for their members. This includes the NEA (the National Education Association). Therefore, you'd think they'd want to get as many children into schools as possible. This would increase the need for teachers and ensure their ongoing demand.

Regardless of where you stand on the abortion issue, a pro-life stance would be logical for the NEA, whereas their pro-choice position hurts their members by decreasing the number of teaching jobs.

If we assume an average class size of twenty-five students, every twenty-five abortions represent the loss of one teaching job—for thirteen years. When you consider the tens of millions of abortions in the United States since 1971, we've lost about *25 million years of teaching jobs*.

The NEA's pro-choice position is as ridiculous as the UAW (United Auto Workers union) promoting bicycle riding and public transportation. That would certainly never fly with the autoworkers, so why do teachers let their union get away with something equally detrimental to their jobs?

What Does Pro-Life Mean?

Ask someone who is pro-life what that means, and they will say that they stand against abortion. True, but what else? If pressed, they may also mention opposition to euthanasia.

But this seems a lot like someone claiming to be a music lover who listens to only one type of music—how limiting. Can anyone truly be a music lover if they experience only a small segment of all things musical?

To truly be pro-life means to affirm *all of life* and seek to improve the condition of *all people.*

As such, pro-life means not only protecting the unborn and terminally ill but also addressing homelessness, unemployment, AIDS, poverty, prejudice, healthcare, social injustice, mass incarceration, immigration, war, slavery, genocide—and anything else that relates to life and living.

These are all important issues to address. These are truly pro-life concerns.

No one can address all these pro-life issues. Even focusing on one can quickly overwhelm our abilities and zap our energy. But that doesn't give us an excuse to do nothing. Therefore, if we are pro-life—and even if we aren't—we must act to affirm the value of all life and do something to help those who struggle.

We can't help everyone, but we can help some of them. Even helping one will make a difference for that person.

Set the Prisoners Free

Sojourners magazine once cited three sobering facts about the state of the prison system in the United States.

First, 7.4 million people were under the control of the US criminal justice system in 2007. I'm not sure what they mean by *under control*. I assume it means incarcerated and those on parole. This is about 2 percent of the population, a shocking number. Compared with the rest of the world, 7.4 million incarcerated people is disproportionate to our population.

Next, 67 percent of people released from prison are rearrested within three years.

The number of repeat offenders in prison is substantial. The question is, how much does incarceration contribute to recidivism? More to the point, would crime decrease if we kept first-time offenders of nonviolent crimes out of prison? The environment is another factor, and in many cases, released prisoners return to the same environment they were in before they were arrested. That certainly doesn't help. Economics is another factor, which leads us to the last statistic.

Of the people in jail in 2002, 83.5 percent earned less than $2,000 a month prior to their arrest. Certainly, economic pressure is a factor in criminal activity. Interestingly, a $2,000-a-month threshold is quite a bit more than the poverty level, which the US Census Bureau put at $9,183 a year ($765 per month) for a single person in 2002, and in 2019, $12,490 per year ($1,041 per month).

Two thousand dollars a month equates to an hourly wage of about $12.50, quite a bit higher than the current minimum wage in the United States—though some states and cities legislate higher rates.

This all suggests that viable employment, at an appropriate wage, is part of the solution to lower crime and incarceration rates. One of the things that Jesus came to do was to help the prisoners (Luke 4:18). Shouldn't we do the same?

What can we do to keep people out of jail, decrease their chance of returning, and help them if they're there?

These are huge questions that lack simple answers. We can begin our search by asking God for direction. Then do an online search for "end mass incarceration" or "lower recidivism rates." Also check out "Facts for the Fatherless" in the next section.

Facts for the Fatherless

Relevant magazine wrote that about one-third of kids in the United States are living in a home without a father.

How sad.

Even more shocking are the ramifications. Children without fathers present in their lives are
- five times more likely to live in poverty;
- five times more likely to commit crimes;
- nine times more likely to drop out of school; and
- twenty times more likely to end up in prison.

Fatherlessness is an epidemic. It strains children. Fatherless boys struggle to figure out how to be a good man and a dad because they lack good examples to follow.

"Ninety-four percent of the prison population is male, 85 percent of which are without fathers," said Donald Miller, best-selling author and founder of The Mentoring Project. This is a sobering reality.

To do something to help fatherlessness children, check out thementoringproject.org and bbbs.org.

Clean Water

I sometimes feel a bit guilty for watering my lawn.

You see, as I dump hundreds of gallons of pure, clean water on my yard, over a billion people on this planet have no clean water to drink. I would gladly forgo my lawn watering ritual if it would somehow quench the thirst of those with parched throats. But any water sacrifice I make here does nothing to satiate those who are thirsty in developing countries.

Even so, there are ways to help. Countless organizations provide inexpensive, simple water filtration units to those who only have access to dirty, germ-laden, and disease-infested water. Even a small donation can provide a safe source of water to those in need. Other organizations drill wells in areas lacking nearby surface water. Wells are more expensive, but they can serve hundreds of people for many years.

Doing an online search for "provide clean drinking water" results in millions of matches. Surely one of those organizations is a good fit for you.

So go ahead and water your lawn. Just remember to do your part to *water* thirsty people too.

Feed the Hungry

When I was a child, my mother told me to eat all the food on my plate because there were starving children in India.

Young me thought, *Just send them my food. I'm full and don't want any more.* As a tiny lad, I imagined placing my unwanted food in the mailbox for the kids in India. Unfortunately, viable solutions aren't so simple.

Not only are there starving children halfway around the world (and a plethora of organizations who provide sponsorship opportunities), there are also hungry people in our local communities. Some are homeless, relying on homeless shelters and food kitchens for their daily food. A couple of bucks will provide a meal for one of them. The results can be even more significant in feeding the hungry in impoverished developing countries, where a few cents can provide a basic meal.

So I can eat at a moderately-priced restaurant or feed ten people at the local shelter or nourish one hundred people in a developing country.

Think about this every time you go out to eat.

Do Something

We've covered a lot of serious needs. The sheer number is paralyzing. Even the scope of need in one of these areas can overwhelm us.

But we don't need to address them all. We can't.

However, we can pick one item, become passionate about it, and dedicate our time/money to help. I have. And in that one area, I can make a difference. Find your area, and you, too, can make someone's life a little better—or maybe a lot better.

Then may we hear Jesus say, "Well done, good and faithful servant." (Check out Matthew 25:21.)

Final Thoughts

And whatever you do, whether in word or deed, do it all in the name of the Lord Jesus, giving thanks to God the Father through him (Colossians 3:17).

We have two more topics to address before we wrap up our discussion. These are not items from the so-called secular realm where we seek to reclaim the spiritual within. For these two spiritual items, we need to cling to their spiritual essence and then move to reform our practices of them.

The Bible

All Scripture is God-breathed and is useful for teaching, rebuking, correcting and training in righteousness, so that the servant of God may be thoroughly equipped for every good work (2 Timothy 3:16).

We are spiritual beings.

That is, we are a spirit. We have a soul (our mind, will, and emotions). And we live in a body.

Think about that.

Most people start with the tangible, the body. And for many, that is where they stop. Yet others may acknowledge that they have a soul too. But for them to add the aspect of spirit is a stretch.

Though this idea of body, soul, and spirit may seem enlightened—and it is—it's also backward. We must start with the idea of spirit, then acknowledge the existence of our souls, and last add in our temporary residence of the body.

In the Bible, Paul recognizes these three facets of our being. He also lists their order of importance. Paul writes, "May your whole spirit, soul, and body be kept blameless" (1 Thessalonians 5:23).

That is: We are a spirit. We have a soul. And we live in a body.

When we view this trio from the perspective that all things are spiritual, it starts to make sense. Yes, everything is spiritual.

However, not everything that is spiritual is good.

I repeat, not everything that's spiritual is good.

There can be good spirituality, bad spirituality, and inconsequential spirituality. To guide us in pursuing the good kind and avoiding the rest, we need to test our understanding of spirituality through the lens of the Bible. We need a biblical basis. The Bible should be our guide in determining a spiritual perspective that's both positive and productive. A spirituality that's not supported by the Bible is one that's suspect and potentially dangerous.

That's why the Bible—and only the Bible—must stand as the basis of our faith. We can't mix and match world religions—embracing some elements and discarding others—to form a spiritual practice that feels good to us.

Well, we can. But that manmade religion won't save us. It may make us feel good now, but it could doom us for eternity. The risk is huge.

That's why I study the Bible. When I was fourteen, I read the entire Bible that summer. (It takes only about eighty hours for the average adult to read the Bible through.) I've continued to read and study the Bible almost every day of my adult life. I've never looked back.

As I read and study the Bible, I share it with others. I blog about it, have a website dedicated to it (ABibleADay.com), and write books about it.

To help you embrace the Bible as your spiritual basis, some of my books may help. Consider:

- *Women of the Bible: The Victorious, the Victims, the Virtuous, and the Vicious*
- *Friends and Foes of Jesus: Explore How People in the New Testament React to God's Good News*
- *Dear Theophilus: A 40-Day Devotional Exploring the Life of Jesus through the Gospel of Luke (a prequel to Dear Theophilus, Acts)*
- *Dear Theophilus, Acts: 40 Devotional Insights for Today's Church*

And I plan to write about thirty more books about the Bible.

The point is: Read the Bible. Use it to guide your spiritual practices and draw you to God, both now and for eternity.

What about Church?

> *And let us consider how we may spur one another on toward love and good deeds, not giving up meeting together, as some are in the habit of doing, but encouraging one another—and all the more as you see the Day approaching (Hebrews 10:24–25).*

This verse doesn't tell us to go to church every Sunday—despite what some preachers claim. It's a command to hang out with other Christians, to form a spiritual community. This may be church, or it may be something different, something radically different—a new kind of church. Church 2.0.

I go to church. Every week. My whole life. I rarely miss a Sunday. I don't say this to brag. I say this to confess. Much of my time going to church has been empty, draining, and void of substance. Too often, I wonder why I go.

I don't go for the music or the message. I go for the people. I go to seek a brief chance for meaningful community before and after the service. At times I find spiritual community in other places too. And when I do, these gatherings become church for me.

Yet I persist in attending one of today's church services each Sunday.

I crave spiritual community. My spirit needs it. My soul requires it. This is how God created me (and you): to desire meaningful community.

Whether you go to church, have dropped out of church, or embrace a nontypical church experience, I encourage you to pursue a meaningful spiritual community. Wait, *encourage* isn't imperative enough. I urge you. I beg you. I implore you to find meaningful spiritual community. And once you do, grab onto it, and don't let go.

Having a meaningful spiritual community will make all the difference in your life and relationships—with others and with God.

Just as I write about the Bible, I also write about church. I blog about church and publish books about church. If you're interested, consider reading the following:

- *52 Churches: A Yearlong Journey Encountering God, His Church, and Our Common Faith*
- *95 Tweets: Celebrating Martin Luther in the 21st Century*
- *More Than 52 Churches* (a sequel to 52 Churches)

The Last Word

Now all has been heard; here is the conclusion of the matter: Fear God and keep his commandments, for this is the duty of all mankind (Ecclesiastes 12:13).

Amen.

Discussion Questions

1. What parts of your life do you consider spiritual activities?
2. What parts do you consider secular?
3. What do you think of Peter's idea that every aspect of life has a spiritual component?
4. God blesses us with family (though some might say he stuck us with them). What can you do to spiritually encourage your loved ones?
5. How can you make your holidays a time to celebrate God?
6. How is God part of the changing seasons, both in your environment and your life?
7. In what ways can you celebrate God through his creation?
8. How does working the land (farming, gardening, or landscaping) connect you with God?
9. We can't control the weather, but we can be in awe of the God who does. How can you worship him through the weather? All kinds of weather?
10. What does it mean for you to rule over the animals God made (see Genesis 1:26)?

11. How does caring for your body affect you spiritually?
12. God gave us work (jobs, tasks, and assignments), but do you thank him for them? What if it's work you don't like?
13. In what ways can you understand your handling of money as a spiritual issue?
14. How can you embrace travel as spiritual?
15. What are some ways you can celebrate yourself and one another as unique creations that God made?
16. How might your areas of competence have a spiritual component?
17. How can making the world a better place be a spiritual activity?
18. How do the Bible and church tie into your pursuit of spirituality?
19. What can you do today to embrace yourself and one another as spiritual beings?
20. What should you do to change your perspective from a spiritual-secular divide into embracing all of life as spiritual?

Bonus Content:

What Does Postmodern Mean?

In talking with a twenty-something friend, I toss out the word *postmodern*. His ears perk up. He asks what it means.

"You're postmodern," I say without giving it much thought. (Turns out I was right.)

"I know," he says and then sighs. "That's what people tell me, but what does it mean?"

"First, there's one aspect of postmodernity that doesn't fit you," I clarify. "Most postmodern thinkers do not accept that there is absolute truth. To them all things are relative. The only thing they accept with absolute certainty is that there are no absolutes." (Don't think about this too long, it will give you a headache.)

"The rest of postmodernism seems to fit you." I pause to corral my thoughts before continuing. "In general, postmodern people value relationships and relish experiences. For them, the 'journey is the reward.' They want work that is fulfilling and allows them to make a difference in the world, but they insist on maintaining a balance between work and their personal lives. Money doesn't mean as much to them as a *modern* person, and they tend not to be materialistic. They are decidedly non-religious, but they are open to the supernatural and engaging in spiritual discussions."

He agrees with me that he is mostly postmodern. "What about you?" he asks.

Younger people tend to be postmodern thinkers, and older people tend to be modern thinkers. This isn't a life-stage phenomenon, but a lifelong mindset. "Being on the tail end of the baby boom generation, I should be modern, like most people my age (and older). But I skew toward postmodern."

He smiles.

I guess that's why we get along so well.

* * *

At the beginning of this book, I mentioned that people decided to divide their lives into the physical and the spiritual, segregating the tangible from the supernatural. This is the result of modern thinking. It sprouted in the 1500s, lasted about five centuries, and sparked the Age of Enlightenment.

Before that, premodern people (and the ancient peoples before them) saw everything as spiritual. To them, no divide existed between the physical and the supernatural. To them, everything was spiritual.

Then there were 500 years of modernity, which tried to ignore—even squelch—matters of faith.

Now, along comes postmodern people. Seeing the emptiness of modern thinking, postmodern thinkers (mostly millennials and younger) are moving past the errors of modernity. Many of them are more like premodern people than modern people. This is because they are open to spiritual matters—not religion, mind you, which they hate, but spirituality—which they pursue to give purpose and meaning to their lives.

We can help.

We can have spiritual discussions with them.

We can guide them to a Bible-based spirituality.

Acknowledgments

I salute the following:

God, who calls me and equips me to write about the kingdom of God.

My bride, who without complaint gives me the time and space to write.

Shara Anjaynith Cazon, my loyal assistant, who does some of my other work so I have more time to write.

The Kalamazoo Christian Writers, who offer support and encouragement.

Joanna Penn, who mentors me from afar about writing and publishing.

And you, who read this book. May God speak to you in everything. After all, all things are spiritual.

Thank you for following my ministry of words.

About Peter DeHaan

Peter DeHaan wants to change the world one word at a time.

He writes about biblical spirituality for a postmodern world. His books and blog posts discuss God, the Bible, and church, geared toward spiritual seekers and church dropouts.

Peter DeHaan, PhD, urges Christians to push past the status quo and reexamine their practices. Many people feel church let them down, and Peter seeks to encourage them as they search for a place to belong. But he's not afraid to ask tough questions or make religious people squirm.

Peter earned a PhD degree from Trinity College of the Bible and Theological Seminary, awarded "with high distinction."

A lifelong student of the Bible, Peter wrote the 700-page website ABibleADay.com to encourage people to explore the Bible, the greatest book ever written.

His popular blog, at PeterDeHaan.com, addresses biblical spirituality, often with a postmodern twist.

Connect with him on Goodreads, Twitter, Facebook, YouTube, Instagram, Pinterest, and LinkedIn, all accessible from his website, PeterDeHaan.com.

Check out Peter's other books:
The Dear Theophilus series:
- *Dear Theophilus: A 40-Day Devotional Exploring the Life of Jesus through the Gospel of Luke*
- *Dear Theophilus, Acts: 40 Devotional Insights for Today's Church*
- *Dear Theophilus, Isaiah: 40 Prophetic Insights about Jesus, Justice, and Gentiles*
- *Dear Theophilus, Minor Prophets: 40 Prophetic Teachings about Unfaithfulness, Punishment, and Hope*
- *Dear Theophilus, Job*

The 52 Churches series:
- *52 Churches: A Yearlong Journey Encountering God, His Church, and Our Common Faith*
- *The 52 Churches Workbook: Becoming a Spiritual Community that Matters*
- *More Than 52 Churches: The Journey Continues* (a sequel to *52 Churches*)
- *The More Than 52 Churches Workbook*

The Bible Bios series:
- *Women of the Bible: The Victorious, the Victims, the Virtuous, and the Vicious*
- *Friends and Foes of Jesus: Explore How People in the New Testament React to God's Good News*

Other books:
- *95 Tweets: Celebrating Martin Luther in the 21st Century*
- *How Big is Your Tent? A Call for Christian Unity, Tolerance, and Love*

Be the first to hear about Peter's new books and receive updates when you sign up at PeterDeHaan.com/updates

www.ingramcontent.com/pod-product-compliance
Lightning Source LLC
Chambersburg PA
CBHW071306110526
44591CB00010B/790